MODERN CANADIAN DOUBLED DIE VARIETIES

FIRST EDITION

by
John O'Connor
Author & Editor

COPYRIGHT & DISCLAIMER

MODERN CANADIAN DOUBLED DIE VARIETIES
First Edition

WRITTEN & PUBLISHED BY:
John O'Connor

Copyright © 2023 John O'Connor
All rights reserved.

Compliance with Canadian copyright laws requires that no part of Modern Canadian Doubled Die Varieties, First Edition, including charts, illustrations, listings, or photographs, be reproduced without written permission from the author. The reference list contains external links with information belonging to the website or individual cited, which may also be protected under copyright laws. As such, copying this information without proper written consent is strictly prohibited. Please note, the author has received written consent from experts, authors, websites, collectors, and members of the Coin Community Forum to reference their posts, photos, or listings in the reference list found in Modern Canadian Doubled Die Varieties, First Edition.

DISCLAIMER:

The author, John O'Connor, of Modern Canadian Doubled Die Varieties, First Edition, has taken all necessary measures to ensure the accuracy of the written information. However, he cannot be held responsible for any errors or omissions that may have occurred. It's important to note that the 57 listings in this catalogue contain examples that are not all in uncirculated condition. Most of the examples were difficult to find, discover, or acquire over a 5-year period of searching. As a result, the overall grades of the examples included may vary.

For permissions not relating to the reference list:

CCF Username: JohnWayne007
Website: www.mcddv.ca
Direct Email: jw.numismatics@outlook.com

ISBN: 978-1-7770888-1-1

INTRODUCTION

For more than 50 years, collectors and variety hunters have often overlooked doubled die varieties due to how scarce most of them are. Canadian numismatic publications rarely mention them because collectors, experts, and roll hunters are simply unaware of their existence, until now.

The First Edition of Modern Canadian Doubled Die Varieties is a comprehensive catalogue that showcases 57 listings and over 100 detailed images of doubled die examples from 1941 to 2022 and covers five denominations: 1¢, 5¢, 10¢, $1, and $2.

In addition, the catalogue contains a reference list of 173 examples from 1941 to 2022 across all several denominations, making it ideal for both new and experienced collectors, as well as variety hunters. The catalogue explains how these varieties occur, why they can be scarce, and how to distinguish between common forms of worthless doubling and authentic doubled die varieties.

When collectors find doubled die examples on Canadian coins intended for circulation or mint sets, they typically want to get them authenticated and attributed by a reputable grading company. However, attribution services for doubled die varieties on Canadian coins are seemingly non-existent due to a lack of proper documentation and research.

Doubled die varieties will normally fetch a fair premium depending on the date, denomination, and overall condition. For example, the 1967 Canadian small cent featuring an impressive doubled die obverse with D.G. REGINA and the Queen's crown doubled can easily fetch upwards of $300 CAD or more at auction when in uncirculated condition. Recently, grading companies have started recognizing and attributing the 1967 one cent doubled die obverse as a true die variety, making them even more valuable to collectors.

Due to how difficult it is to find doubled dies, the First Edition of Modern Canadian Doubled Die Varieties does not focus on the grade of the coins that may be included in the listings. The main focus of this catalogue is to spread awareness amongst collectors of what to look for and how to correctly recognize these oftentimes scarce die varieties. Although some examples showcased are circulated, they are still in fact genuine doubled die varieties that occurred during the die hubbing process when the working hub transfers the obverse or reverse die design onto the surface of the working dies.

REFERENCE LIST SOURCES & SPECIAL MENTIONS

I would like to express my appreciation and say thank you to the individuals and websites acknowledged below for permission to reference listing numbers, photographs, and coin community forum posts. Their individual contributions were instrumental in the creation of the extensive reference list and some of the included listings featured in the First Edition of Modern Canadian Doubled Die Varieties. - *John O'Connor*

Roger Paulen:
For supplying examples, images for listings, and his knowledge of doubled dies.

Ken Potter:
For permission to reference his VCR Numbers and website.
https://koinpro.tripod.com/Articles/canada_1974__vars.htm

Tanner Scott:
For permission to reference his doubled die listings and website.
www.crdievarieties.com

Jonny Gauvin:
For supplying high quality images to help create listings and to be referenced.

Jakob Miller:
For permission to reference CCF posts, images, and supplying images for listings.

Coin Community:
For being one of the best numismatic families around.
www.coincommunity.com

Coins and Canada:
For permission to reference listings, numbers, and images.
www.coinsandcanada.com

CCF - Fourmack:
For permission to reference his CCF posts, and images.

CCF - Ondiwave:
For permission to reference his CCF posts, and images.

CCF - Numidan:
For permission to reference his CCF posts, and images.

Buying & Selling Canadian Error & Variety Coins

Roger Paulen

PO Box 67008, Westboro RPO
Ottawa, ON K2A 4E4
sherwood.park.pennies@gmail.com
613-894-0386

ebay: SPP-Ottawa

Coin Community Family
Education is the key to collector success!

Whether you are a new or experienced collector, joining the Coin Community is a great way to connect with others who share your passion for Canadian numismatic errors, varieties, tokens, bills, and grading standards. As a member, you can engage in conversations with like-minded collectors, dealers, authors, and experts. Best of all, membership is free and highly recommended.

Canadian Coins and Colonial Tokens:
https://www.coincommunity.com/forum/forum.asp?FORUM_ID=32

Canadian Variety and Error Coins:
https://www.coincommunity.com/forum/forum.asp?FORUM_ID=139

Canadian Coin Grading:
https://www.coincommunity.com/forum/forum.asp?FORUM_ID=138

Canadian Commemoratives and Non-Circulating Coinage (NCLT):
https://www.coincommunity.com/forum/forum.asp?FORUM_ID=144

Canadian Bank Notes & Paper Money (Errors, Varieties, Grading):
https://www.coincommunity.com/forum/forum.asp?FORUM_ID=166

To access the website or become a member, simply scan the QR code using your cellular device's camera which will direct you to www.coincommunity.com.

Disclaimer: If the QR code does not work, expires, or leads to an incorrect website, the author and the coin community will not be held accountable for any technical issues related to the faulty QR code.

ABBREVIATIONS

Short Form	Meaning	Short Form	Meaning
RCM	Royal Canadian Mint	NC	Non Coloured
CCF	Coin Community Forum	C	Coloured
DDO	Doubled Die Obverse	T1 to T99+	Type 1 to Type 99+
DDR	Doubled Die Reverse	BU	Brilliantly Uncirculated
DDD	Die Deterioration Doubling	UNC	Uncirculated
MD	Machine Doubling	RPD	Re-Punched Date
REV	Reverse	GC	Grey Cup
OBV	Obverse	OL	Olympic Loon
S5	Small 5	PNT	Pointed
CLW	Claw	BLT	Blunt
NSC	No Security Feature	L	Leaf
SC	Security Feature	R	Regular
QEII	Queen Elizabeth II	Incuse	Indented, Sunken, Impression
VI	Georgivs VI	P	Copper Plated Steel

Inside the First Edition of Modern Canadian Doubled Die Varieties, readers will come across the use of abbreviations. To understand the abbreviations used, refer to the chart provided above.

It's relatively easy to understand the listing numbers as each number is comprised of 5 to 6 specific details, below is a breakdown to help understand them accurately.

$$\underset{(1)}{\boxed{12}} - \underset{(2)}{\boxed{\text{QEII}}} - \underset{(3)}{\boxed{1\text{D}}} - \underset{(4)}{\boxed{\text{DDO}}} - \underset{(5)}{\boxed{\text{T1}}} - \underset{(6)}{\boxed{\text{SC}}}$$

1. Last 2 digits of the date.
2. **QEII** (Queen Elizabeth II) or **VI** (Georgivs VI).
3. Denomination **1C** (1 Cent), **5C** (5 Cents), **10C** (10 Cents), **1D** (1 Dollar) etc.
4. **DDO** (Doubled Die Obverse) or **DDR** (Doubled Die Reverse).
5. **T1** (Type 1), **T2** (Type 2), **T3** (Type 3) etc.
6. Extra info when needed such as a Security (**SC**) version, or extended variety type like a doubled claw (**CLW**).

INDEX

Copyright & Disclaimer 3
Introduction 4
   Reference List Sources & Special Mentions 5
   Abbreviations 8
   Understanding the Die Hubbing Process 12
   How Master Die Doubling can Occur - Common 13
   How Doubled Die Varieties can Occur - Uncommon 14
   Comparing MD, DDD & Doubled Die Varieties 15
   How to Identify Doubled Die Features 16
ONE CENT DOUBLED DIE LISTINGS 17
   1941 - Georgivs VI - 1¢ - DDO - Type 1 18
   1941 - Georgivs VI - 1¢ - DDO - Type 3 - HP 20
   1949 - Georgivs VI - 1¢ - DDO 22
   1951 - Georgivs VI - 1¢ - DDO - Type 2 24
   1957 - Elizabeth II - 1¢ - DDO 26
   1964 - Elizabeth II - 1¢ - DDR - Type 1 - Bud 28
   1964 - Elizabeth II - 1¢ - DDR - Type 3 - Spine 30
   1964 - Elizabeth II - 1¢ - DDR - Type 4 - Spine 32
   1967 - Elizabeth II - 1¢ - DDO 34
   1972 - Elizabeth II - 1¢ - DDR - Type 1 - Bud 36
   1972 - Elizabeth II - 1¢ - DDR - Type 2 - Bud 38
   1975 - Elizabeth II - 1¢ - DDO 40
   1976 - Elizabeth II - 1¢ - DDO - Type 1 42
   1976 - Elizabeth II - 1¢ - DDO - Type 2 44
   1994 - Elizabeth II - 1¢ - DDO - Type 1 46
   2008 - Elizabeth II - 1¢ - DDR 48
   One Cent Doubled Die Summary 50
FIVE CENT DOUBLED DIE LISTINGS 51
   1965 - Elizabeth II - 5¢ - DDR - Type 1 - Claw 52
   1965 - Elizabeth II - 5¢ - DDR - Type 2 - Small 5 54
   1966 - Elizabeth II - 5¢ - DDR - Type 1 - Claw 56
   1972 - Elizabeth II - 5¢ - DDR - Type 1 - Claw 58

1984 - Elizabeth II - 5¢ - DDR - Claw 60
2012 - Elizabeth II - 5¢ - DDO 62
2012 - Elizabeth II - 5¢ - DDR - Claw 64
2013 - Elizabeth II - 5¢ - DDO - Type 1 66
2013 - Elizabeth II - 5¢ - DDO - Type 2 68
2013 - Elizabeth II - 5¢ - DDO - Type 3 70
2013 - Elizabeth II - 5¢ - DDO - Type 4 72
Five Cent Doubled Die Summary 74

TEN CENT DOUBLED DIE LISTINGS 75
1951 - Georgivs VI - 10¢ - DDR - Type 1 76
1951 - Georgivs VI - 10¢ - DDR - Type 2 78
1952 - Georgivs VI - 10¢ - DDR 80
1955 - Elizabeth II - 10¢ - DDO 82
1968 - Elizabeth II - 10¢ - DDO 84
1973 - Elizabeth II - 10¢ - DDO 86
1974 - Elizabeth II - 10¢ - DDR - Type 2 88
2005-P - Elizabeth II - 10¢ - DDR 90
2012 - Elizabeth II - 10¢ - DDO - Type 1 92
2012 - Elizabeth II - 10¢ - DDO - Type 2 94
2012 - Elizabeth II - 10¢ - DDR - Type 1 96
2012 - Elizabeth II - 10¢ - DDR - Type 2 98
Ten Cent Doubled Die Summary 100

ONE DOLLAR DOUBLED DIE LISTINGS 101
2012 - Elizabeth II - $1 - DDO - Type 1 - Security 102
2012 - Elizabeth II - $1 - DDO - Type 2 - Security 104
2012 - Elizabeth II - $1 - DDO - Type 3 - Security 106
2012 - Elizabeth II - $1 - DDO - Type 4 - Security 108
2012 - Elizabeth II - $1 - DDO - Type 5 - Security 110
2012 - Elizabeth II - $1 - DDR - Type 1 - Security 112
2012 - Elizabeth II - $1 - DDR - Type 2 - Security 114
2012 - Elizabeth II - $1 - DDO + DDR - Type 1 - Security 116
2012 - Elizabeth II - $1 - DDO - Olympic Loon 118
2012 - Elizabeth II - $1 - DDO - Grey Cup 120

2014 - Elizabeth II - $1 - DDR - Olympic Loon 122
2021 - Elizabeth II - $1 - DDR -Type 1 - Klondike Non Coloured 124
2021 - Elizabeth II - $1 - DDR -Type 2 - Klondike Non Coloured 126
2021 - Elizabeth II - $1 - DDR - Klondike Coloured 128
2022 - Elizabeth II - $1 - DDR - Security 130
One Dollar Doubled Die Summary 132
TWO DOLLAR DOUBLED DIE LISTINGS 133
2012 - Elizabeth II - $2 - DDO - Type 1 - Security 134
2012 - Elizabeth II - $2 - DDO - Type 2 - Security 136
2012 - Elizabeth II - $2 - DDO - HMS Shannon 138
Two Dollar Doubled Die Summary 140
DOUBLED DIE REFERENCE LIST 141
1 Cent: 1941 - 2008 142
5 Cents: 1947 - 2020 144
10 Cents: 1951 - 2012 146
25 Cents: 1953 - 1972 147
50 Cents: 1943 - 1996 147
1 Dollar: 1945 - 2022 148
2 Dollars: 2011 - 2021 151

UNDERSTANDING THE DIE HUBBING PROCESS

— Below is a small scale visualization of how the master hub transfers the coins design to the master die, from the master die to the working hub, then from the working hub to a working die by the use of a process known as multi-stage hubbing.

Although a single master hub is typically used, the use of one or two master dies and multiple working hubs allows for a diverse range of obverse and reverse working dies to be created. For illustrative purposes, the process has been simplified to include only one master hub, one master die, one working hub, and one reverse working die.

It is important to note that the reverse design showcased in the illustration is a digital representation created solely for educational purposes, and is not an actual reverse design used for Canadian coins.

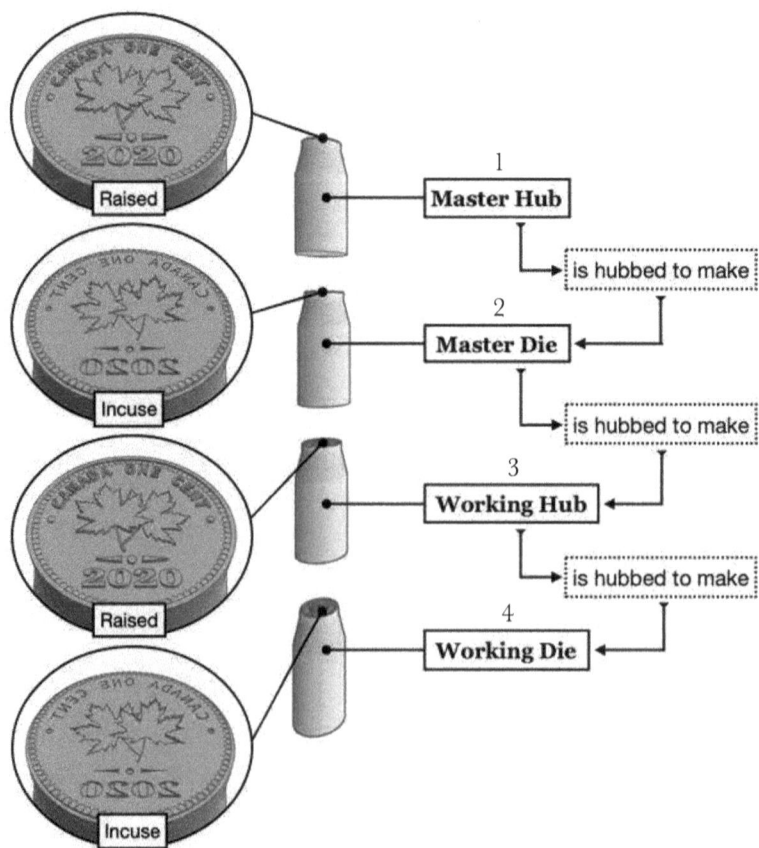

HOW MASTER DIE DOUBLING CAN OCCUR - COMMON

— Master die doubling can sometimes occur during the multi-stage hubbing process when the **master hub** (1) leaves an additional hubbing impression on one or more of the blank **master dies** (2) that is slightly offset, tilted, or misaligned from the first hubbing impression early in the die making process before the working dies that strike coins have been made.

It is important to highlight that when master die doubling happens it becomes common for that date and denomination and should only be used as a means of learning. This is because the doubling is transferred from the master die to the working hub and then on to every working die that is used to strike coins. Consequently, every coin that is struck by the working dies will feature master die doubling.

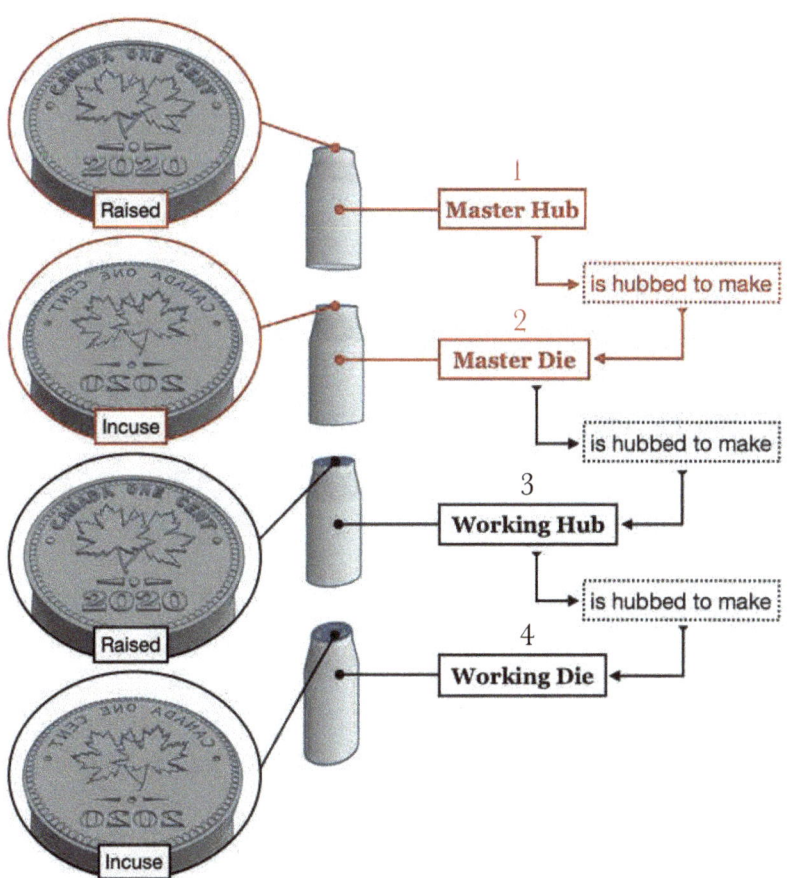

HOW DOUBLED DIE VARIETIES CAN OCCUR - UNCOMMON

— Multi-stage hubbing is a process that can cause doubled die varieties to occur, this happens when the **working hub** (3) leaves an additional hubbing impression on one or more of the blank **working dies** (4) that is not correctly aligned with the first hubbing impression. Due to this, design details can become rotated, pivoted, tilted, or offset, creating a noticeable gap between the two hubbing impressions.

Unlike master die doubling that affects every single working die, only a handful of working dies may be affected with a doubled die variety that occurred when the working hub leaves an additional hubbing impression that is not correctly aligned with the first hubbing impression, while the rest of the working dies will be normal.

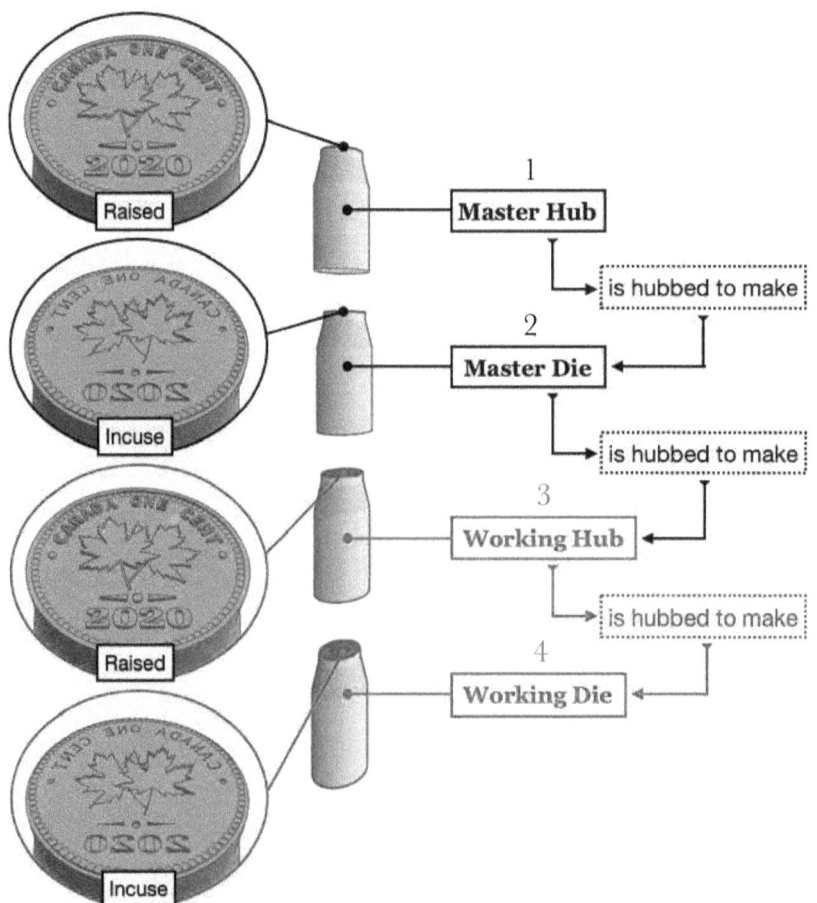

COMPARING MD, DDD & DOUBLED DIE VARIETIES

- **Machine Doubling (MD):** A common mechanical issue that can frequently occur when the obverse or reverse working dies become loose, shifts, or vibrates during the strike. This can cause the device edges of the working die to cut into the design details on either side of the coin on its way back up from the strike (red highlighted areas). Machine doubling reduces the overall size of the raised letters or design details on the surface of a coin, giving the impression of being doubled when it is not. This common form of doubling should not carry a premium.

- **Die Deterioration Doubling (DDD):** A common occurrence during the overall life span of the obverse and reverse working dies, this is not considered to be an error, or a variety. After many strikes and an immense amount of pressure, the working dies can begin to wear down and deteriorate causing details like letters or numbers to seem larger, or distorted (red highlighted areas). This can give a false impression of being doubled, however it is only the result of an over used working die that exceeded its life expectancy and does not normally carry a premium.

- **Doubled Die Obverse, or Doubled Die Reverse (DDO or DDR):** Doubled die varieties occur during the die hubbing process when the working dies are being made, before any coin has been struck. If a shift, tilt, or rotation happens during the second hubbing impression and it is not correctly aligned with the first hubbing impression (the green highlighted area), the working dies can feature doubled design details, lettering, and numbers. A doubled die will carry a premium depending on the date, the denomination, the overall grade, and the mintage.

HOW TO IDENTIFY DOUBLED DIE FEATURES

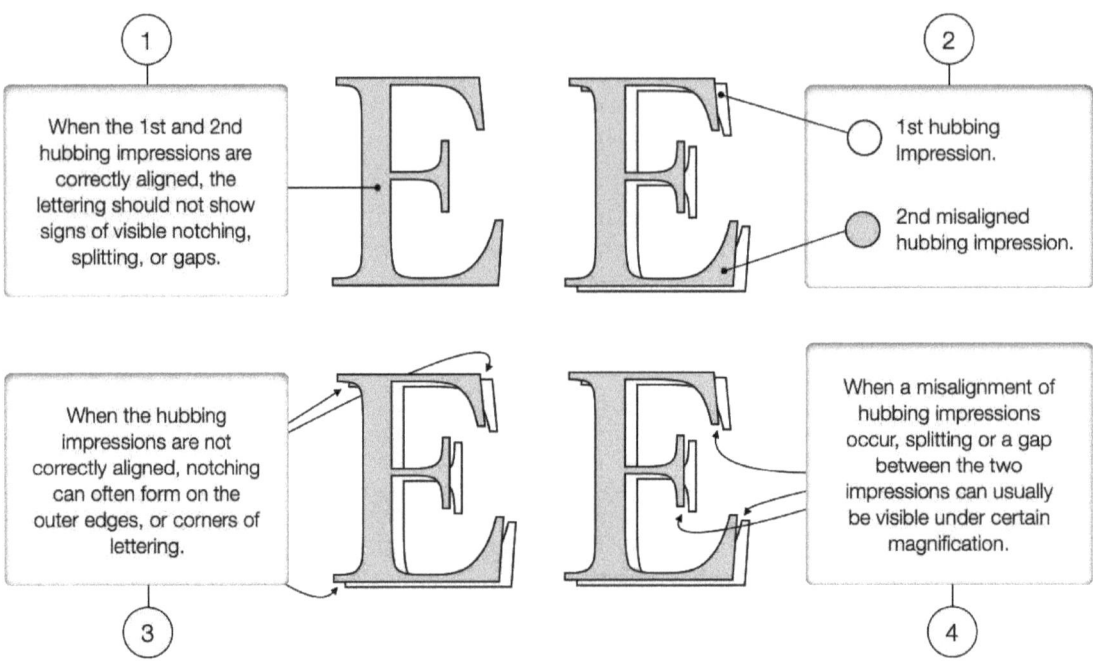

Identifying a doubled die variety on a coin depends on its overall condition and the visibility of the separation or gap between the first and second hubbing impressions. The appearance of doubled die varieties can vary, with the second hubbing impression shifting or tilting in different directions. However, they will always display notching, splitting, or gaps between the first and second hubbing impressions.

While there are various types of reverse doubled die varieties, collectors tend to prefer those with well-pronounced splitting, gaps, or notching between the first and second hubbing impressions. Learning how to identify these varieties is an essential skill for variety collectors, regardless of their level of experience. Doubled die varieties on Canadian coins can be highly rewarding, with some examples being scarce and carrying a fair premium depending on their grade.

The loon dollars for example, have produced some of the most impressive doubled die obverse and reverse varieties seen on Canadian coins since the 1974 nickel dollar doubled die varieties. Even circulated rolls of Canadian one-dollar coins often contain at least one example of a genuine doubled die, and boxes from the bank have produced many examples, including those listed in Modern Canadian Doubled Die Varieties.

ONE CENT DOUBLED DIE LISTINGS

— Charts for the one cent doubled die listings include mintages, designers and engravers information, compositions, weight, and previously sold prices when applicable. If no prices have been established yet they will be left blank (—). Prices included should be treated as estimates only and are in Canadian currency (CAD).

Doubled Die Reverse (DDR) - Examination Areas:

When looking for doubled die reverse examples on one cent coins, it is good practice to examine the following for any signs of doubled design details that should not be present on dates from 1937 to 2012.

- **BUD** - Most common area to find a DDR.
- **SPINE** - Located on the right side of the bud.
- **DATE** - Numbers feature splits or notching (for 1970, this is master die doubling).
- **CANADA** - Letters feature notching (for 1970, this is master die doubling).

Doubled Die Obverse (DDO) - Examination Areas:

When looking for doubled die obverse examples on one cent coins, split serifs and notching can be found on one letter, or all of the letters in the following obverse legends.

- **GEORGIVS VI - D:G: - REX - ET - IND:IMP:** - From 1937 to 1947.
- **GEORGIVS VI - DEI - GRATIA - REX** - From 1948 to 1952.
- **ELIZABETH II - D.G. REGINA** - From 1952 to 2012.
- **Queen's CROWN & JEWELS** - For 1965 to 1978 portraits only.

Doubled die varieties on the Canadian one cent coins are becoming harder to find due to these iconic coins being discontinued in May of 2012 and pulled from circulation in February of 2013 to be recycled.

Some of Canada's one cent coins have a very low mintage and with the existing population slowly being removed since 2013, it will ultimately cause doubled die examples found on coins with already low mintages to become even more scarce year after year.

1941 - GEORGIVS VI - 1¢ - DDO - TYPE 1

The 1941 Doubled Die Obverse Type 1 example shown here was discovered and photographed by John O'Connor in 2019 while searching circulated bank rolls in Kawartha Lakes, Ontario.

ONE CENT   PAGE 19

EXAMINATION NOTES:

41-VI-1C-DDO-T1

All of the obverse legends are doubled, with split serifs that can be found on the following letters.

- "**E**" in GEORGIVS, REX & ET
- "**T**" in ET
- "**I**" in GEORGIVS
- "**V**" in GEORGIVS
- "**S**" in GEORGIVS

Currently the only known example to date. Finding an example higher than AU would likely carry a fair premium.

1941 Georgivs VI - Doubled Die Obverse - Type 1							
DATE	**EF-40**	**AU-50**	**MS-60**	**MS-62**	**MS-63**	**MS-64**	**MS-65**
1¢-1941-VI-Normal Obv.	5.00	8.00	10.50	40.00	49.80	84.50	550.00
41-VI-1C-DDO-T1	—	—	—	—	—	—	—
Mintage	56,336,011						

Contents:	**Weight:**	**Dimensions:**	**Engravers & Designers:**	**Edge/Rim:**	**Magnetism:**	**Die Axis:**
95.5% Copper, 0.3% Tin, 1.5% Zinc	3.24 Grams	19.05 mm x 1.65 mm	**Obv:** T.H.Paget **Rev:** G.E. Kruger-Gray	Smooth	Not Magnetic	↑↑

* Please Note: Due to market fluctuation the prices included in this chart are estimates only.

1941 - GEORGIVS VI - 1¢ - DDO - TYPE 3 - HP

The 1941 Doubled Die Obverse Type 3 doubled HP example shown here was found and photographed by John O'Connor in 2019 while searching circulated bank rolls in Kawartha Lakes, Ontario.

EXAMINATION NOTES:

41-VI-1C-DDO-T3-HP

The minor doubled HP variety requires the use of magnification between 50x - 100x to fully examine and the use of a microscope would be ideal, split serifs can be found on the bottom of the designer initials located below the obverse portrait.

- "**H**" Shows a visible split on the lower right.
- "**P**" Visible splits on the lower left and right.

Although minor, the doubled HP variety is a good example to find when learning how to identify a genuine doubled die.

1941 Georgivs VI - Doubled Die Obverse - Type 3 - HP Only							
DATE	EF-40	AU-50	MS-60	MS-62	MS-63	MS-64	MS-65
1¢-1941-VI-Normal Obv.	5.00	8.00	10.50	40.00	49.80	84.50	550.00
41-VI-1C-DDO-T3-HP	—	—	—	—	—	—	—
Mintage	56,336,011						
Contents:	Weight:	Dimensions:	Engravers & Designers:		Edge/Rim:	Magnetism:	Die Axis:
95.5% Copper, 0.3% Tin, 1.5% Zinc	3.24 Grams	19.05 mm x 1.65 mm	**Obv:** T.H.Paget **Rev:** G.E. Kruger-Gray		Smooth	Not Magnetic	↑↑

* Please Note: Due to market fluctuation the prices included in this chart are estimates only.

1949 - GEORGIVS VI - 1¢ - DDO

The 1949 Doubled Die Obverse example shown here was discovered and photographed by John O'Connor in 2019 while searching circulated bank rolls in Kawartha Lakes, Ontario.

EXAMINATION NOTES:

49-VI-1C-DDO

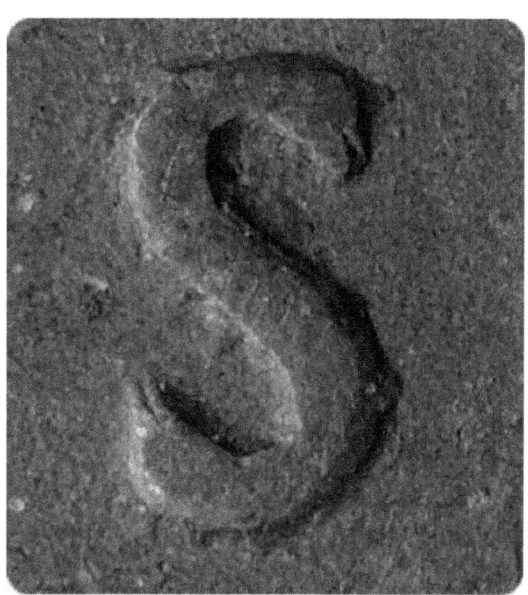

The example shown here is in fairly rough shape, however splitting can be found on the following letters in the obverse legends.

- "**I**" in GEORGIVS
- "**V**" in GEORGIVS
- "**S**" in GEORGIVS
- "**G**" in GRATIA
- "**R**" in GRATIA

This listing is for the 1949 "A Points between Denticles" variety.

1949 Georgivs VI - Doubled Die Obverse							
DATE	**EF-40**	**AU-50**	**MS-60**	**MS-62**	**MS-63**	**MS-64**	**MS-65**
1¢-1941-VI-Normal Obv.	2.00	4.50	8.00	11.00	13.50	42.00	55.00
49-VI-1C-ABD-DDO	—	—	—	—	—	—	—
Mintage	33,128,933						
Contents:	**Weight:**	**Dimensions:**	**Engravers & Designers:**		**Edge/Rim:**	**Magnetism:**	**Die Axis:**
95.5% Copper, 0.3% Tin, 1.5% Zinc	3.24 Grams	19.05 mm x 1.65 mm	**Obv:** T.H.Paget **Rev:** G.E. Kruger-Gray		Smooth	Not Magnetic	↑↑

* Please Note: Due to market fluctuation the prices included in this chart are estimates only.

1951 - GEORGIVS VI - 1¢ - DDO - TYPE 2

The 1951 Doubled Die Obverse Type 2 example shown here was discovered and photographed by John O'Connor in 2019 while searching circulated bank rolls in Kawartha Lakes, Ontario.

EXAMINATION NOTES:

51-VI-1C-DDO-T2

The 1951 small cent doubled die obverse Type 2 shows distinctive splitting on the tips of the letters that make up the obverse legends DEI, GRATIA, and REX.

Similar to the scarce doubled die variety reported to Ken Potter by Alan Herbert in 1981 referred to as Type 1, when comparing the two, it is evident that the Type 2 example shown here goes in an opposite direction.

Type 1 is far more elusive compared to Type 2, while both are considered to be semi-key dates.

1951 Georgivs VI - Doubled Die Obverse - Type 2							
DATE	EF-40	AU-50	MS-60	MS-62	MS-63	MS-64	MS-65
1951 KGVI - Normal Obv.	4.00	6.50	8.00	10.00	16.00	40.00	120.00
51-VI-1C-DDO-T2	26.00	38.00	50.00	65.00	70.00	115.00	225.00
Mintage	80,430,379						

Contents:	Weight:	Dimensions:	Engravers & Designers:	Edge/Rim:	Magnetism:	Die Axis:
98% Copper, 0.5% Tin, 1.5% Zinc	3.24 Grams	19.05 mm x 1.65 mm	**Obv:** T.H.Paget **Rev:** G.E. Kruger-Gray	Smooth	Not Magnetic	↑↑

* Please Note: Due to market fluctuation the prices included in this chart are estimates only.

1957 - ELIZABETH II - 1¢ - DDO

The 1957 Doubled Die Obverse example shown here was discovered and photographed by John O'Connor in 2019 while searching circulated bank rolls in Kawartha Lakes, Ontario.

EXAMINATION NOTES:

57-QEII-1C-DDO

Split serifs can be found on the following letters in the obverse legends.

- "**E**" in ELIZABETH, DEI & REGINA
- "**L**" in ELIZABETH
- "**Z**" in ELIZABETH
- "**D**" in DEI
- "**I**" in DEI

Although this example is minor compared to most, doubled dies that are genuine are still worth noting regardless of if they are minor or major.

1957 Queen Elizabeth II - Doubled Die Obverse								
DATE	EF-40	AU-50	MS-60	MS-62	MS-63	MS-64	MS-65	
1957 QEII - Normal Obv.	5.00	6.50	8.00	10.00	12.50	14.00	26.00	
57-QEII-1C-DDO	—	—	—	—	—	—	—	
Mintage	100,601,792							
Contents	Weight:	Dimensions:	Engravers:	Designers:	Edge/Rim:	Magnetism:	Die Axis:	
98% Copper, 0.5% Tin, 1.5% Zinc	3.24 Grams	19.05 mm x 1.65 mm	Obv & Rev: Thomas Shingles	Obv: Mary Gillick Rev: G.E. Kruger-Gray	Smooth	Not Magnetic	↑↑	

* Please Note: Due to market fluctuation the prices included in this chart are estimates only.

1964 - ELIZABETH II - 1¢ - DDR - TYPE 1 - BUD

The 1964 Doubled Die Reverse Type 1 Bud example shown here was photographed by John O'Connor in 2022 and was sent from Roger Paulen in 2021 to include in this Catalogue.

EXAMINATION NOTES:

64-QEII-1C-DDR-T1-BUD

For the 1964 small cents there are more than one type of extra bud variety that can be found while searching the reverse.

This example shows remanence of a smaller bud created from the first hubbing impression protruding directly north from the larger bud created from the final second hubbing impression.

Surprisingly this date and denomination is one that has an abundance of doubled die reverse examples featuring doubled buds, and doubled spines.

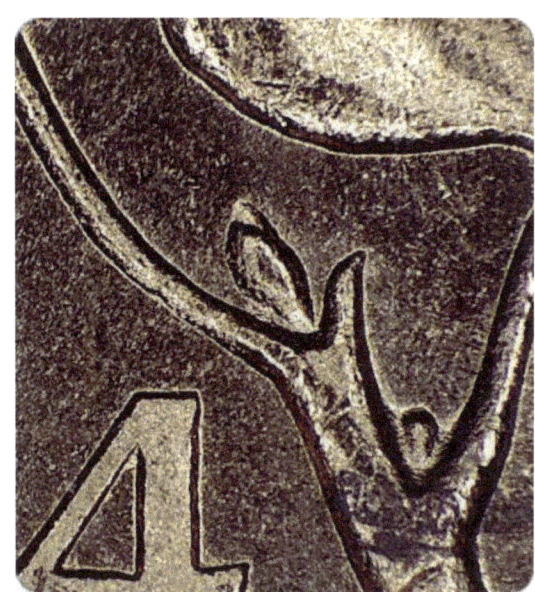

1964 Queen Elizabeth II - Doubled Die Reverse - Type 1 - Bud							
DATE	EF-40	AU-50	MS-60	MS-62	MS-63	MS-64	MS-65
1964 QEII - Normal Rev.	3.50	5.00	6.50	8.00	10.00	12.50	15.00
64-QEII-1C-DDR-T1-BUD	—	—	—	—	—	—	—
Mintage	484,655,322						
Contents:	Weight:	Dimensions:	Engravers:	Designers:	Edge/Rim:	Magnetism:	Die Axis:
98% Copper, 0.5% Tin, 1.5% Zinc	3.24 Grams	19.05 mm x 1.65 mm	Obv & Rev: Thomas Shingles	Obv: Mary Gillick Rev: G.E. Kruger-Gray	Smooth	Not Magnetic	↑↑

* Please Note: Due to market fluctuation the prices included in this chart are estimates only.

1964 - ELIZABETH II - 1¢ - DDR - TYPE 3 - SPINE

The 1964 Doubled Die Reverse Type 3 Spine example shown here was photographed by John O'Connor in 2022 while searching circulated bank rolls in Kawartha Lakes, Ontario.

EXAMINATION NOTES:

64-QEII-1C-DDR-T3-SPINE

The 1964 extra spine shown here is one of the most impressive doubled spines on this date, with a well raised first impression of the spine directly beside the bud.

For years the extra spine varieties that can be found on more than one date of Canadian 1 Cent coins was controversial and subject to speculations of being a possible die crack, or a tooling mark.

A die crack or tooling mark is not likely to repeat itself across more than one year, while a doubled die can look identical on more than one year.

1964 Queen Elizabeth II - Doubled Die Reverse - Type 3 - Spine								
DATE	EF-40	AU-50	MS-60	MS-62	MS-63	MS-64	MS-65
1964 QEII - Normal Rev.	3.50	5.00	6.50	8.00	10.00	12.50	15.00
64-QEII-1C-DDR-T3-SP	—	—	—	—	—	—	—
Mintage	484,655,322							
Contents:	Weight:	Dimensions:	Engravers:	Designers:	Edge/Rim:	Magnetism:	Die Axis:
98% Copper, 0.5% Tin, 1.5% Zinc	3.24 Grams	19.05 mm x 1.65 mm	Obv & Rev: Thomas Shingles	Obv: Mary Gillick Rev: G.E. Kruger-Gray	Smooth	Not Magnetic	↑↑

*Please Note: Due to market fluctuation the prices included in this chart are estimates only.

1964 - ELIZABETH II - 1¢ - DDR - TYPE 4 - SPINE

The 1964 Doubled Die Reverse Type 4 Spine example shown here was photographed by John O'Connor in 2022 and was sent from Roger Paulen in 2021 to include in this Catalogue.

EXAMINATION NOTES:

64-QEII-1C-DDR-T4-SPINE

The 1964 extra spine variety is similar to the extra bud varieties. There are more than one version of the extra spine variety and searching 1964 small cents will likely bring forth more versions that have not been seen before.

Although this example shown here is somewhat minor, it does feature an obvious extra spine that occurred from the first hubbing impression hiding between the bud and spine that was left from the second hubbing impression.

1964 Queen Elizabeth II - Doubled Die Reverse - Type 4 - Spine							
DATE	EF-40	AU-50	MS-60	MS-62	MS-63	MS-64	MS-65
1964 QEII - Normal Rev.	3.50	5.00	6.50	8.00	10.00	12.50	15.00
64-QEII-1C-DDR-T4-SP	—	—	—	—	—	—	—
Mintage	484,655,322						
Contents:	Weight:	Dimensions:	Engravers:	Designers:	Edge/Rim:	Magnetism:	Die Axis:
98% Copper, 0.5% Tin, 1.5% Zinc	3.24 Grams	19.05 mm x 1.65 mm	Obv & Rev: Thomas Shingles	Obv: Mary Gillick Rev: G.E. Kruger-Gray	Smooth	Not Magnetic	↑↑

* Please Note: Due to market fluctuation the prices included in this chart are estimates only.

1967 - ELIZABETH II - 1¢ - DDO

The 1967 Doubled Die Obverse example shown here was found and photographed by John O'Connor in 2019 while searching circulated bank rolls in Kawartha Lakes, Ontario.

ONE CENT

EXAMINATION NOTES:

67-QEII-1C-DDO

The 1967 Doubled Die Obverse has become quite scarce when it comes to finding one in circulation. Originally discovered by a collector named Robert Wilharm in 1977.

- The obverse legend D.G. REGINA features a distinctive spread between the doubled letters.
- Doubled Crown & Jewels.
- Doubled Eye (retina).

Higher grade examples of this doubled die variety will carry a hefty premium of $300 CAD or more.

The 1967 doubled die obverse on the cover is MS-62, however, a circulated example is easier to photograph as details show more clearly, that is why a circulated example was used for this listing.

Normal

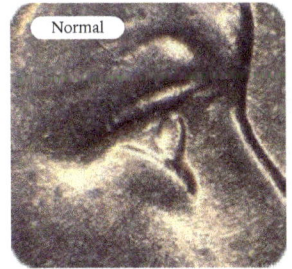
Normal

Doubled

Doubled

1967 Queen Elizabeth II - Doubled Die Obverse								
DATE	EF-40	AU-50	MS-60	MS-62	MS-63	MS-64	MS-65
1967 QEII - Normal Obv.	3.50	4.00	6.50	8.00	10.00	12.50	15.00
67-QEII-1C-DDO	35.00	50.00	80.00	95.00	190.00	260.00	450.00
Mintage	345,140,645						
Contents:	Weight:	Dimensions:	Engravers & Designers:		Edge/Rim:	Magnetism:	Die Axis:
98% Copper, 0.5% Tin, 1.5% Zinc	3.24 Grams	19.05 mm x 1.65 mm	**Obv:** Arnold Machin **Rev:** Alex Colville		Smooth	Not Magnetic	↑↑

* Please Note: Due to market fluctuation the prices included in this chart are estimates only.

1972 - ELIZABETH II - 1¢ - DDR - TYPE 1 - BUD

The 1972 Doubled Die Reverse Type 1 Bud example shown here was found and photographed by John O'Connor in 2019 while searching circulated bank rolls in Kawartha Lakes, Ontario.

EXAMINATION NOTES:

72-QEII-1C-DDR-T1-BUD

Like the 1964 extra bud varieties, the 1972 small cent also features this type of doubled die. When searching small cents from the 70's it is always good practice to examine the bud and spine area.

The example shown here features a small bud from the first hubbing impression directly above the bud from the second hubbing impression going north.

Extra bud varieties can be minor, or major and will usually require a loupe or microscope to properly examine.

1972 Queen Elizabeth II - Doubled Die Reverse - Type 1 - Bud							
DATE	EF-40	AU-50	MS-60	MS-62	MS-63	MS-64	MS-65
1972 QEII - Normal Rev.	1.00	2.50	4.00	5.25	8.50	12.50	18.00
72-QEII-1C-DDR-T1-BUD	—	—	—	—	—	—	—
Mintage	451,304,591						
Contents:	Weight:	Dimensions:		Engravers & Designers:	Edge/Rim:	Magnetism:	Die Axis:
98% Copper, 0.5% Tin, 1.5% Zinc	3.24 Grams	19.05 mm x 1.65 mm		**Obv:** Arnold Machin **Rev:** G.E. Kruger-Gray	Smooth	Not Magnetic	↑↑

* Please Note: Due to market fluctuation the prices included in this chart are estimates only.

1972 - ELIZABETH II - 1¢ - DDR - TYPE 2 - BUD

The 1972 Doubled Die Reverse Type 2 Bud example shown here was found and photographed by John O'Connor in 2019 while searching circulated bank rolls in Kawartha Lakes, Ontario.

EXAMINATION NOTES:

72-QEII-1C-DDR-T2-BUD

This example of the 1972 small cent referred to as Type 2 features an extra bud, but also features small remanence of an extra spine. Extra bud and extra spine varieties can be in various locations around the main bud, including the spine.

A loupe or microscope is recommenced when searching for extra bud or spine varieties as details can sometimes be too small for the naked eye to see.

Regardless of size all genuine doubled die varieties are collectable, especially in high grade.

1972 Queen Elizabeth II - Doubled Die Reverse - T2 - Bud								
DATE	EF-40	AU-50	MS-60	MS-62	MS-63	MS-64	MS-65
1972 QEII - Normal Rev.	1.00	2.50	4.00	5.25	8.50	12.50	18.00
72-QEII-1C-DDR-T2-BUD	—	—	—	—	—	—	—
Mintage	451,304,591						
Contents:	Weight:	Dimensions:	Engravers & Designers:		Edge/Rim:	Magnetism:	Die Axis:
98% Copper, 0.5% Tin, 1.5% Zinc	3.24 Grams	19.05 mm x 1.65 mm	**Obv:** Arnold Machin **Rev:** G.E. Kruger-Gray		Smooth	Not Magnetic	↑↑

* Please Note: Due to market fluctuation the prices included in this chart are estimates only.

1975 - ELIZABETH II - 1¢ - DDO

The 1975 Doubled Die Obverse example shown here was found and photographed while searching circulated bank rolls by John O'Connor in May 2020 in Kawartha Lakes, Ontario.

EXAMINATION NOTES:

75-QEII-1C-DDO

The 1975 Doubled Die Obverse was discovered by Tanner Scott in December 2019 and is listed on his website www.crdievarieties.com. Split serifs can be found on the following letters in the obverse legends.

- "**E**" in ELIZABETH, DEI & REGINA
- "**L**" in ELIZABETH
- "**I**" in ELIZABETH
- "**Z**" in ELIZABETH
- "**A**" in ELIZABETH
- "**B**" in ELIZABETH
- "**N**" in REGINA

1975 Queen Elizabeth II - Doubled Die Obverse									
DATE	EF-40	AU-50	MS-60	MS-62	MS-63	MS-64	MS-65
1975 QEII - Normal Obv.	1.00	2.50	4.00	5.25	8.50	12.50	18.00
75-QEII-1C-DDO	—	—	—	—	—	—	—
Mintage	642,618,000						
Contents:	Weight:	Dimensions:	Engravers & Designers:	Edge/Rim:	Magnetism:	Die Axis:
95.5% Copper, 0.3% Tin, 1.5% Zinc	3.24 Grams	19.05 mm x 1.65 mm	**Obv:** T.H.Paget **Rev:** G.E. Kruger-Gray	Smooth	Not Magnetic	↑↑

* Please Note: Due to market fluctuation the prices included in this chart are estimates only.

1976 - ELIZABETH II - 1¢ - DDO - TYPE 1

The 1976 Doubled Die Obverse Type 1 example shown here was discovered and photographed by John O'Connor in early 2020 while searching circulated bank rolls in Kawartha Lakes, Ontario.

EXAMINATION NOTES:

76-QEII-1C-DDO-T1

The 1976 doubled die obverse Type 1 small cent features split serifs visible on the following letters in the obverse legends.

- "**E**" in ELIZABETH, DEI & REGINA
- "**L**" in ELIZABETH
- "**I**" in ELIZABETH
- "**Z**" in ELIZABETH
- "**A**" in ELIZABETH
- "**B**" in ELIZABETH
- "**N**" in REGINA

1976 Queen Elizabeth II - Doubled Die Obverse - Type 1								
DATE	**EF-40**	**AU-50**	**MS-60**	**MS-62**	**MS-63**	**MS-64**	**MS-65**
1976 QEII - Normal Obv.	1.00	2.50	4.00	5.25	8.50	12.50	18.00
76-QEII-1C-DDO-T1	—	—	—	—	—	—	—
Mintage	701,122,890							
Contents:	**Weight:**	**Dimensions:**	**Engravers & Designers:**		**Edge/Rim:**	**Magnetism:**	**Die Axis:**
98% Copper, 0.5% Tin, 1.5% Zinc	3.24 Grams	19.05 mm x 1.65 mm	**Obv:** Arnold Machin **Rev:** G.E.Gruger-Gray		Smooth	Not Magnetic	↑↑

* Please Note: Due to market fluctuation the prices included in this chart are estimates only.

1976 - ELIZABETH II - 1¢ - DDO - TYPE 2

The 1976 Doubled Die Obverse Type 2 example shown here was discovered and photographed by John O'Connor in early 2020 while searching circulated bank rolls in Kawartha Lakes, Ontario.

EXAMINATION NOTES:

76-QEII-1C-DDO-T2

1976 doubled die obverse Type 2 features split serifs visible on the following letters in the obverse legends going in the opposite direction as **76-QVII-1C-DDO-T1**.

- "**E**" in ELIZABETH, DEI & REGINA
- "**L**" in ELIZABETH
- "**I**" in ELIZABETH
- "**Z**" in ELIZABETH
- "**A**" in ELIZABETH
- "**B**" in ELIZABETH
- "**N**" in REGINA

1976 Queen Elizabeth II - Doubled Die Obverse - Type 2							
DATE	EF-40	AU-50	MS-60	MS-62	MS-63	MS-64	MS-65
1976 QEII - Normal Obv.	1.00	2.50	4.00	5.25	8.50	12.50	18.00
76-QEII-1C-DDO-T2	—	—	—	—	—	—	—
Mintage	701,122,890						
Contents:	Weight:	Dimensions:	Engravers & Designers:		Edge/Rim:	Magnetism:	Die Axis:
98% Copper, 0.5% Tin, 1.5% Zinc	3.24 Grams	19.05 mm x 1.65 mm	**Obv:** Arnold Machin **Rev:** G.E.Gruger-Gray		Smooth	Not Magnetic	↑↑

* Please Note: Due to market fluctuation the prices included in this chart are estimates only.

1994 - ELIZABETH II - 1¢ - DDO - TYPE 1

The 1994 Doubled Die Obverse Type 1 example shown here was discovered and photographed by John O'Connor in 2019 while searching circulated bank rolls in Kawartha Lakes, Ontario.

EXAMINATION NOTES:

94-QEII-1C-DDO-T1

Splitting can be found on the following letters in the obverse legends and doubled beads on necklace.

- "**R**" in REGINA
- "**E**" in RGINA
- "**G**" in REGINA
- "**I**" in REGINA
- "**N**" in REGINA
- "**A**" in REGINA

A die chip is visible below the Queen's necklace and it can be used as a die marker when searching for this doubled die variety.

1994 Queen Elizabeth II - Doubled Die Obverse - Type 1								
DATE	EF-40	AU-50	MS-60	MS-62	MS-63	MS-64	MS-65
1994 QEII - Normal Obv.	0.50	1.00	3.00	4.50	8.00	11.25	24.00
94-QEII-1C-DDO-T1	—	—	—	—	—	—	—
Mintage	639,516,000						
Contents:	Weight:	Dimensions:	Engravers:	Designers:	Edge/Rim:	Magnetism:	Die Axis:
98% Copper, 0.5% Tin, 1.5% Zinc	3.24 Grams	19.05 mm x 1.45 mm	Obv & Rev: Thomas Shingles	Obv: Mary Gillick Rev: G.E. Kruger-Gray	Smooth	Not Magnetic	↑↑

* Please Note: Due to market fluctuation the prices included in this chart are estimates only.

2008 - ELIZABETH II - 1¢ - DDR

The 2008 Doubled Die Reverse example shown here was discovered and photographed by John O'Connor in 2021 while searching circulated bank rolls in Kawartha Lakes, Ontario.

ONE CENT PAGE 49

EXAMINATION NOTES:

08-QEII-1C-DDR

The 2008 small cent shown here features a minor, but distinctive first hubbing impression hidden behind the last two digits in the date (highlighted in red).

Specifically on the top right side of the loops in the number 8 and the top right of the loop on the number 0.

Finding this minor doubled die reverse variety in circulation might be difficult compared to searching BU rolls as the condition can affect the ability to see the doubled digits under magnification.

2008 Queen Elizabeth II - Doubled Die Reverse								
DATE	EF-40	AU-50	MS-60	MS-62	MS-63	MS-64	MS-65	
2008 QEII - Normal Rev.	0.25	0.50	2.50	4.00	6.50	8.00	12.00	
08-QEII-1C-DDR	—	—	—	—	—	—	—	
Mintage	787,625,000							
Contents:	Weight:	Dimensions:	Engravers & Designers:		Edge/Rim:	Magnetism:	Die Axis:	
98% Copper, 0.5% Tin, 1.5% Zinc	3.24 Grams	19.05 mm x 1.45 mm	**Obv:** Susanna Blunt, Susan Taylor **Rev:** G.E. Kruger-Gray		Smooth	Not Magnetic	↑↑	
* Please Note: Due to market fluctuation the prices included in this chart are estimates only.								

ONE CENT DOUBLED DIE SUMMARY

It's important to note that mintages of one cent coins that were once high, such as the 1941 Canadian one cent coin with a mintage of 56+ million, will eventually decrease significantly over time. As of 2013, the mintage could be closer to 35+ million, depending on how many coins have been removed from circulation.

The Canadian one cent coin was produced in large quantities using multiple working dies, but not all of them will feature a doubled obverse or reverse. As the already low mintage becomes even lower over time, any doubled die varieties that have been discovered or are still out there, can become increasingly scarce.

Common Master Die Doubling Examples to Ignore

The copper plated steel (P) versions of the 2003-P, 2004-P, and 2005-P coins display worthless master die doubling on the obverse near the Queen's ear and earring crease. However, the Plated Zinc versions do not exhibit any doubling.

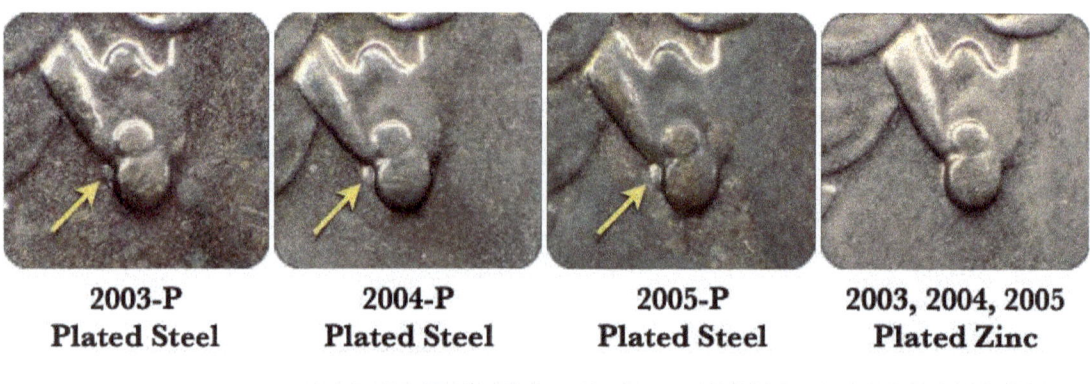

| 2003-P Plated Steel | 2004-P Plated Steel | 2005-P Plated Steel | 2003, 2004, 2005 Plated Zinc |

The 1970 small cent also features master die doubling visible on the numbers in the date, and on the bottom of the letters in CANADA.

1970 - Bottom left tip of "7" split.

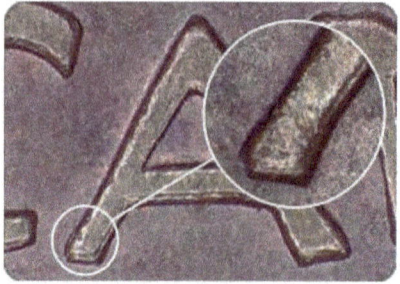

1970 - Notching on bottom left of the "A" in CANADA.

FIVE CENT DOUBLED DIE LISTINGS

— Charts for the five cent doubled die listings include mintages, designers and engravers information, compositions, weight, and previously sold prices when applicable. If no prices have been established yet they will be left blank (—). Prices included should be treated as estimates only and are in Canadian currency (CAD).

Doubled Die Reverse (DDR) - Examination Areas:

1964 to 1966 nickels feature master die doubling on the legends in the outer fields and should be ignored, examine the inner fields for signs of a DDR present.

- **5 CENTS** - Except for 1964 to 1966 as they feature master die doubling (common).
- **LEAVES** - Except for 1964 to 1966 as they feature master die doubling (common).
- **BEAVERS REAR Paw** - Can feature a doubled claw, or claws, from 1942 - 2021.
- **DATE** - Can sometimes feature notching or splitting on the last digit of the date.
- **CANADA** - Except 1964 to 1966 as they feature master die doubling (common).

Doubled Die Obverse (DDO) - Examination Areas:

When looking for doubled die obverse examples on five cent coins, split serifs and notching can be found on one letter, or all of the letters in the following obverse legends.

- **GEORGIVS VI - D:G: - REX - ET - IND:IMP:** - From 1937 to 1947.
- **GEORGIVS VI - DEI - GRATIA - REX** - From 1948 to 1952.
- **ELIZABETH II - D.G. REGINA** - From 1952 to 2022.

Doubled die examples being found on the Canadian 5 cent coins are still relatively new when it comes to widely known examples. There is a fair amount of doubled claw varieties (DDR's) found on the reverse of the coin, but not very many doubled die obverse examples that have been found.

Most of the doubled die obverse varieties have been found on the 2012 and 2013 nickels, for prior years however, there have not been any new discoveries of doubled die obverse varieties to date.

1965 - ELIZABETH II - 5¢ - DDR - TYPE 1 - CLAW

The 1965 Doubled Die Reverse Type 1 Claw example shown here was found and photographed by John O'Connor in 2019 while searching circulated bank rolls in Kawartha Lakes, Ontario.

EXAMINATION NOTES:

65-QEII-5C-DDR-T1-CLW

A doubled claw, also known as an extra claw can be found above the rear paw and directly below the beavers belly.

Extra claw varieties can be in various locations closer to the centre of the reverse design, usually around the rear paw of the beaver.

Fairly high magnification is often needed, however the majority of extra claw varieties can be seen with a simple handheld loupe under 10x to 30x strength.

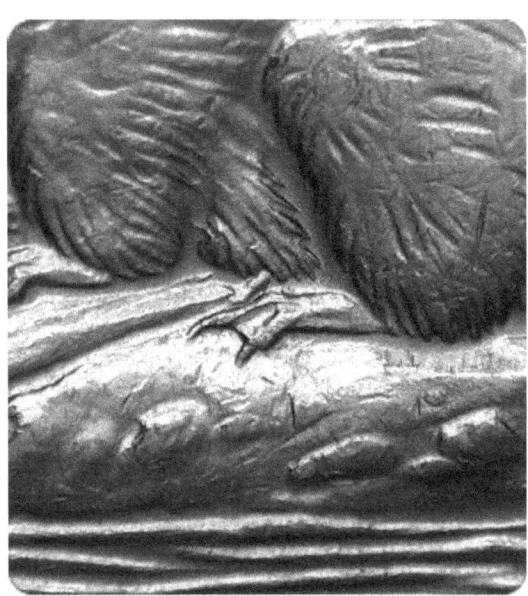

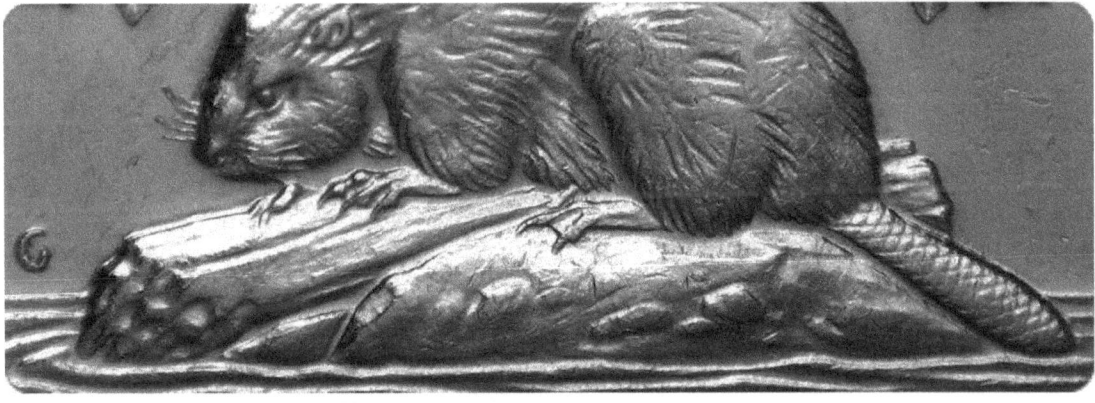

1965 Queen Elizabeth II - Doubled Die Reverse - T1 - Claw							
DATE	EF-40	AU-50	MS-60	MS-62	MS-63	MS-64	MS-65
1965 QEII - Normal Claw	1.00	2.60	6.00	8.50	10.00	14.00	80.00
65-QEII-5C-DDR-T1-CLW	—	—	—	—	—	—	—
Mintage	84,876,018						
Contents:	Weight:	Dimensions:	Engravers & Designers:		Edge/Rim:	Magnetism:	Die Axis:
100% Nickel	4.54 Grams	21.21 mm x 1.7 mm	**Obv:** Arnold Machin, RCM **Rev:** G.E. Kruger-Gray, Thomas Shingles		Smooth	Magnetic	↑↑

* Please Note: Due to market fluctuation the prices included in this chart are estimates only.

1965 - ELIZABETH II - 5¢ - DDR - TYPE 2 - SMALL 5

The 1965 Doubled Die Reverse Type 2 Small 5 example shown here was found and photographed by John O'Connor in 2019 while searching circulated bank rolls in Kawartha Lakes, Ontario.

EXAMINATION NOTES:

65-QEII-5C-DDR-T2-S5

When searching for the 1965 Small 5 nickel with a doubled 5, notching can be found on the 5 of the date. A small 5 has a thin tail and a large upper gap, see "Small 5" vs "Normal 5" photo below.

Doubled Small 5

Small 5 — Normal 5

1965 Queen Elizabeth II - Doubled Die Reverse - Type 2 - Small 5								
DATE	EF-40	AU-50	MS-60	MS-62	MS-63	MS-64	MS-65	
1965 QEII - Normal 5	1.00	2.60	6.00	8.50	10.00	14.00	80.00	
65-QEII-5C-DDR-T2-S5	—	—	—	—	—	—	—	
Mintage	84,876,018							
Contents:	Weight:	Dimensions:	Engravers & Designers:		Edge/Rim:	Magnetism:	Die Axis:	
100% Nickel	4.54 Grams	21.21 mm x 1.7 mm	**Obv:** Arnold Machin, RCM **Rev:** G.E. Kruger-Gray, Thomas Shingles		Smooth	Magnetic	↑↑	

* Please Note: Due to market fluctuation the prices included in this chart are estimates only.

1966 - ELIZABETH II - 5¢ - DDR - TYPE 1 - CLAW

The 1966 Doubled Die Reverse Type 1 Claw example shown here was found and photographed by John O'Connor in 2019 while searching circulated bank rolls in Kawartha Lakes, Ontario.

EXAMINATION NOTES:

66-QEII-5C-DDR-T1-CLW

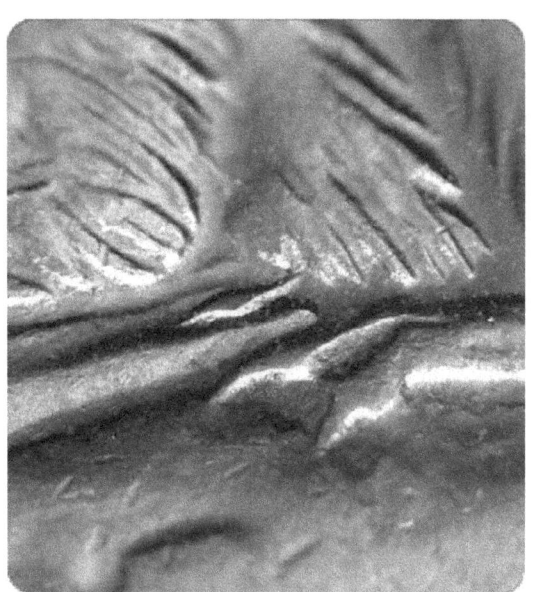

A doubled claw, also known as an extra claw can be found between the front leg and rear paw, directly below the beavers belly. Extra claw varieties are easier to find than most other doubled dies.

With magnification from 10x to 50x the extra claw can easily be seen. There may also be other minor anomalies present such as a skeptical variety commonly referred to as "Eyes" which are really just small die chips on the inside loops of the last two digits in the date "66" that look like retina's looking to the right.

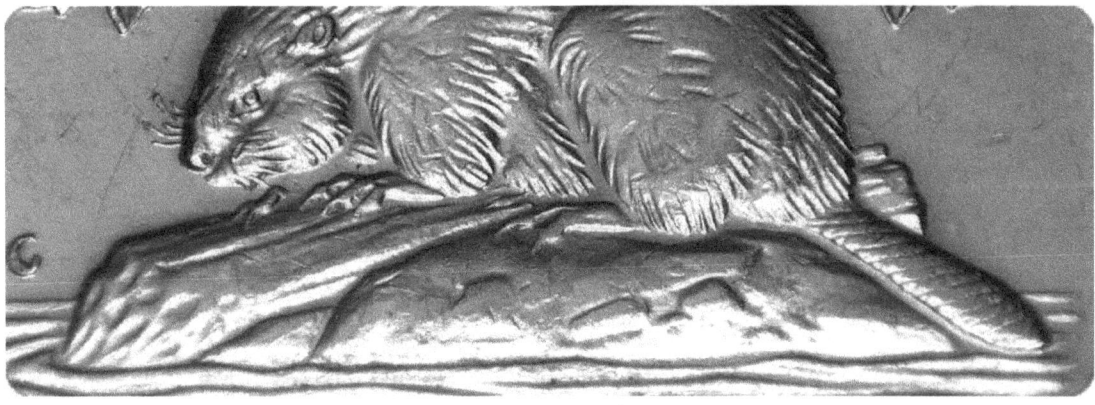

1966 Queen Elizabeth II - Doubled Die Reverse Type 1 - Claw							
DATE	EF-40	AU-50	MS-60	MS-62	MS-63	MS-64	MS-65
1966 QEII - Normal Claw	1.00	2.60	6.00	8.00	12.50	16.00	280.00
66-QEII-5C-DDR-T1-CLW	—	—	—	—	—	—	—
Mintage	27,976,648						
Contents:	Weight:	Dimensions:	Engravers & Designers:		Edge/Rim:	Magnetism:	Die Axis:
100% Nickel	4.54 Grams	21.21 mm x 1.7 mm	**Obv:** Arnold Machin, RCM **Rev:** G.E. Kruger-Gray, Thomas Shingles		Smooth	Magnetic	↑↑

* Please Note: Due to market fluctuation the prices included in this chart are estimates only.

1972 - ELIZABETH II - 5¢ - DDR - TYPE 1 - CLAW

The 1972 Doubled Die Reverse Type 1 Claw example shown here was found and photographed by John O'Connor in 2019 while searching circulated bank rolls in Kawartha Lakes, Ontario.

EXAMINATION NOTES:

72-QEII-5C-DDR-T1-CLW

A doubled claw, also known as an extra claw can be found between the front leg and rear paw directly below the beavers belly.

Hidden directly beneath the belly, these varieties are sometimes hard to notice at first glance as they can sometimes look like part of the log that the beaver is resting on.

Through closer examination of the reverse while using a recommended magnification of 10x to 50x it is obvious that it features an identical impression of the top rear claw.

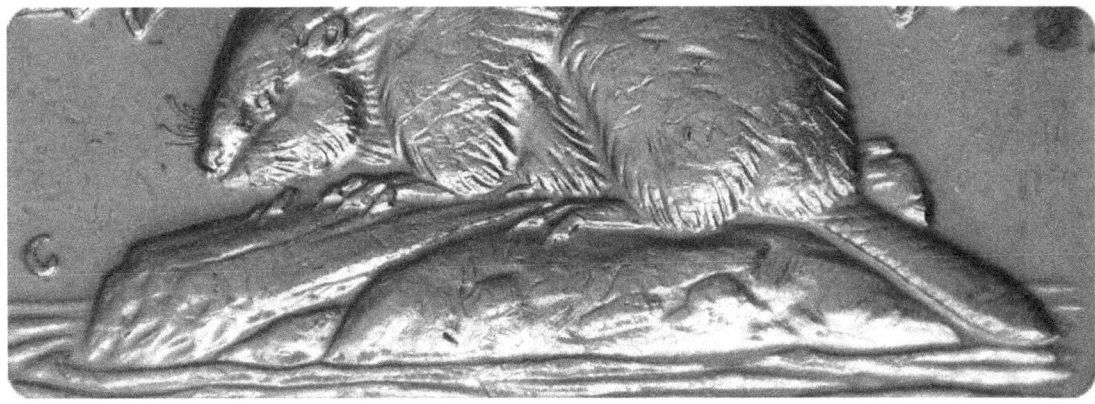

1972 Queen Elizabeth II - Doubled Die Reverse - T1 - Claw							
DATE	EF-40	AU-50	MS-60	MS-62	MS-63	MS-64	MS-65
1972 QEII - Normal Claw	1.00	2.60	5.00	7.00	9.50	16.00	35.00
72-QEII-5C-DDR-T1-CLW	—	—	—	—	—	—	—
Mintage	62,417,387						
Contents:	Weight:		Dimensions:	Engravers & Designers:	Edge/Rim:	Magnetism:	Die Axis:
100% Nickel	4.54 Grams		21.21 mm x 1.7 mm	**Obv:** Arnold Machin, RCM **Rev:** G.E. Kruger-Gray, Thomas Shingles	Smooth	Magnetic	↑↑

* Please Note: Due to market fluctuation the prices included in this chart are estimates only.

1984 - ELIZABETH II - 5¢ - DDR - CLAW

The 1984 Doubled Die Reverse Claw example shown here was found and photographed by John O'Connor in 2019 while searching circulated bank rolls in Kawartha Lakes, Ontario.

EXAMINATION NOTES:

84-QEII-5C-DDR-CLW

A doubled claw, also known as an extra claw can be found between the two claws on the rear paw of the beaver.

Higher grade examples of this doubled die reverse extra claw variety are harder to come by as the majority of them have been found in circulation.

With the use of magnification between 10x to 50x finding a BU example could potentially produce a small premium from the right buyer that collects extra claw doubled die reverse varieties.

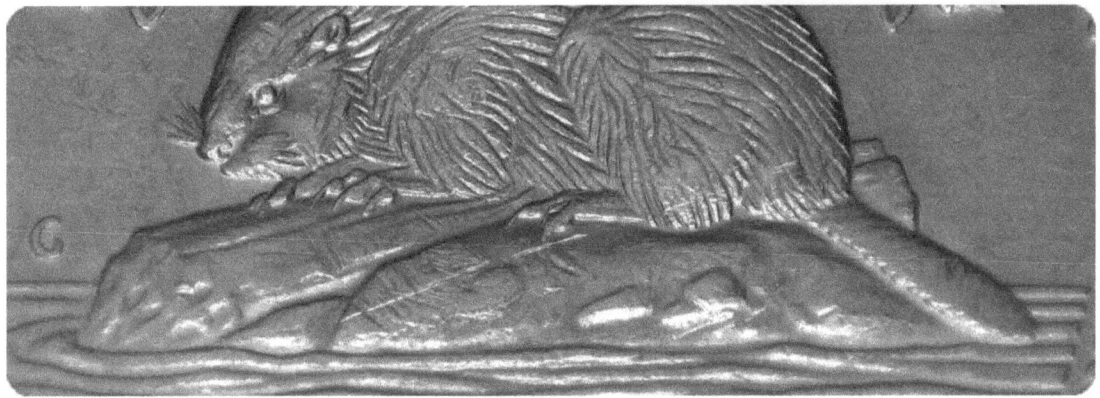

1984 Queen Elizabeth II - Doubled Die Reverse - Claw							
DATE	EF-40	AU-50	MS-60	MS-62	MS-63	MS-64	MS-65
1984 QEII - Normal Claw	1.00	2.60	3.00	4.50	6.00	12.00	80.00
84-QEII-5C-DDR-CLW	—	—	—	—	—	—	—
Mintage	84,088,000						
Contents:	Weight:	Dimensions:		Engravers & Designers:		Edge/Rim:	Magnetism:	Die Axis:
100% Nickel	4.54 Grams	21.21 mm x 1.7 mm		**Obv:** Arnold Machin, Walter Ott **Rev:** G.E. Kruger-Gray, Thomas Shingles		Smooth	Magnetic	↑↑

* Please Note: Due to market fluctuation the prices included in this chart are estimates only.

2012 - ELIZABETH II - 5¢ - DDO

The 2012 Doubled Die Obverse example shown here was found and photographed by John O'Connor in 2019 while searching circulated bank rolls in Kawartha Lakes, Ontario.

EXAMINATION NOTES:

12-QEII-5C-DDO

When searching the obverse of the 2012 nickel for doubled die varieties, one should look for notching on the lower left or right side of each letter in REGINA.

Although seemingly minor, this double die obverse example shows very nice notching and extra thickness of the letters.

The use of magnification can range from 20x to 100x depending on the overall condition of the example being examined.

2012 Queen Elizabeth II - Doubled Die Obverse							
DATE	EF-40	AU-50	MS-60	MS-62	MS-63	MS-64	MS-65
2012 QEII - Normal Obv.	1.00	2.60	5.00	6.25	7.50	8.00	18.00
12-QEII-5C-DDO	—	—	—	—	—	—	—
Mintage	202,944,000						
Contents:	Weight:	Dimensions:	Engravers & Designers:		Edge/Rim:	Magnetism:	Die Axis:
100% Nickel	4.54 Grams	21.21 mm x 1.76 mm	Obv: Arnold Machin, RCM, Rev: G.E. Kruger-Gray, Thomas Shingles		Smooth	Magnetic	↑↑

*Please Note: Due to market fluctuation the prices included in this chart are estimates only.

2012 - ELIZABETH II - 5¢ - DDR - CLAW

The 2012 Doubled Die Reverse Claw example shown here was found and photographed by John O'Connor in 2019 while searching circulated bank rolls in Kawartha Lakes, Ontario.

EXAMINATION NOTES:

12-QEII-5C-DDR-CLW

While searching the 2012 nickels for doubled die obverse examples, looking over the reverse can also be beneficial as sometimes a minor extra claw can also be found.

Not like the typical extra claws shown previously, this example shows an extra second claw directly beside the last claw on the beavers rear paw.

Condition and lighting play a big part in noticing this extra claw, with magnification in the range of 10x to 50x depending on overall condition.

2012 Queen Elizabeth II - Doubled Die Reverse - Claw							
DATE	EF-40	AU-50	MS-60	MS-62	MS-63	MS-64	MS-65
2012 QEII - Normal Claw	1.00	2.60	5.00	6.25	7.50	8.00	18.00
12-QEII-5C-DDR-CLW	—	—	—	—	—	—	—
Mintage	202,944,000						
Contents:	Weight:	Dimensions:		Engravers & Designers:	Edge/Rim:	Magnetism:	Die Axis:
100% Nickel	4.54 Grams	21.21 mm x 1.76 mm		**Obv:** Arnold Machin, RCM **Rev:** G.E. Kruger-Gray, Thomas Shingles	Smooth	Magnetic	↑↑

* Please Note: Due to market fluctuation the prices included in this chart are estimates only.

2013 - ELIZABETH II - 5¢ - DDO - TYPE 1

The 2013 Doubled Die Obverse Type 1 example shown here was found and photographed by John O'Connor in 2019 while searching circulated bank rolls in Kawartha Lakes, Ontario.

EXAMINATION NOTES:

13-QEII-5C-DDO-T1

2013 was a very good year for featuring doubled die obverse varieties of various degrees.

The example shown here referred to as the 2013 doubled die obverse Type 1 features a minor, but distinctive separation between the first hubbing impression and the second hubbing impression.

Underneath the letters in the legend ELIZABETH, notching and minor splitting can be seen between the first and second hubbing impressions, 20x - 50x magnification is recommended.

2013 Queen Elizabeth II - Doubled Die Obverse - Type 1							
DATE	EF-40	AU-50	MS-60	MS-62	MS-63	MS-64	MS-65
2013 QEII - Normal Obv.	1.00	2.60	5.00	6.25	7.50	12.00	24.50
13-QEII-5C-DDO-T1	—	—	—	—	—	—	—
Mintage	78,120,000						
Contents:	Weight:	Dimensions:	Engravers & Designers:		Edge/Rim:	Magnetism:	Die Axis:
94.5% Steel, 3.5% Copper, 2% Nickel	3.95 Grams	21.21 mm x 1.76 mm	Obv: Susanna Blunt, Susan Taylor Rev: G.E. Kruger-Gray, Thomas Shingles		Smooth	Magnetic	↑↑

* Please Note: Due to market fluctuation the prices included in this chart are estimates only.

2013 - ELIZABETH II - 5¢ - DDO - TYPE 2

The 2013 Doubled Die Obverse Type 2 example shown here was found and photographed by John O'Connor in 2019 while searching circulated bank rolls in Kawartha Lakes, Ontario.

EXAMINATION NOTES:

13-QEII-5C-DDO-T2

The 2013 doubled die obverse Type 2 example shown here has an impressive separation between the first and the second hubbing impression.

Clear splitting and visible notching can be found on the letters that make up the obverse legend D.G. REGINA.

Magnification recommendations would be between 10x and 30x for this example by the use of a USB microscope or handheld loupe.

2013 Queen Elizabeth II - Doubled Die Obverse - Type 2							
DATE	EF-40	AU-50	MS-60	MS-62	MS-63	MS-64	MS-65
2013 QEII - Normal Obv.	1.00	2.60	5.00	6.25	7.50	12.00	24.50
13-QEII-5C-DDO-T2	—	—	—	—	—	—	—
Mintage	78,120,000						
Contents:	Weight:	Dimensions:	Engravers & Designers:		Edge/Rim:	Magnetism:	Die Axis:
94.5% Steel, 3.5% Copper, 2% Nickel	3.95 Grams	21.21 mm x 1.76 mm	**Obv:** Susanna Blunt, Susan Taylor **Rev:** G.E. Kruger-Gray, Thomas Shingles		Smooth	Magnetic	↑↑

*Please Note: Due to market fluctuation the prices included in this chart are estimates only.

2013 - ELIZABETH II - 5¢ - DDO - TYPE 3

The 2013 Doubled Die Obverse Type 3 example shown here was found and photographed by John O'Connor in 2019 while searching circulated bank rolls in Kawartha Lakes, Ontario.

EXAMINATION NOTES:

13-QEII-5C-DDO-T3

The example shown here for the 2013 nickel features another impressive doubled die obverse with the second hubbing impression going in a counter-clockwise direction.

Doubled letters are most visible in the obverse legend ELIZABETH II. There are multiple types and directions that the doubled letters can go with visible splitting and notching.

Magnification needed to examine this example is minimal and ranges from 10x to 50x.

2013 Queen Elizabeth II - Doubled Die Obverse - Type 3								
DATE	EF-40	AU-50	MS-60	MS-62	MS-63	MS-64	MS-65
2013 QEII - Normal Obv.	1.00	2.60	5.00	6.25	7.50	12.00	24.50
13-QEII-5C-DDO-T3	—	—	—	—	—	—	—
Mintage	78,120,000						
Contents:	Weight:	Dimensions:	Engravers & Designers:		Edge/Rim:	Magnetism:	Die Axis:
94.5% Steel, 3.5% Copper, 2% Nickel	3.95 Grams	21.21 mm x 1.76 mm	**Obv:** Susanna Blunt, Susan Taylor **Rev:** G.E. Kruger-Gray, Thomas Shingles		Smooth	Magnetic	↑↑

* Please Note: Due to market fluctuation the prices included in this chart are estimates only.

2013 - ELIZABETH II - 5¢ - DDO - TYPE 4

The 2013 Doubled Die Obverse Type 4 example shown here was found and photographed by John O'Connor in 2019 while searching circulated bank rolls in Kawartha Lakes, Ontario.

EXAMINATION NOTES:

13-QEII-5C-DDO-T4

This 2013 doubled die obverse Type 4 example may look somewhat similar to the Type 1 doubled die obverse shown previously.

However, when comparing the Type 1 and the Type 4 doubled die obverse examples together, it is worth noting that Type 4 will show a visible first hubbing impression hidden below the obverse legends D.G. REGINA.

The Type 1 example will only show remanence of the first hubbing impression directly below the letters in the obverse legend ELIZABETH II.

2013 Queen Elizabeth II - Doubled Die Obverse - Type 4							
DATE	EF-40	AU-50	MS-60	MS-62	MS-63	MS-64	MS-65
2013 QEII - Normal Obv.	1.00	2.60	5.00	6.25	7.50	12.00	24.50
13-QEII-5C-DDO-T4	—	—	—	—	—	—	—
Mintage	78,120,000						

Contents:	Weight:	Dimensions:	Engravers & Designers:	Edge/Rim:	Magnetism:	Die Axis:
94.5% Steel, 3.5% Copper, 2% Nickel	3.95 Grams	21.21 mm x 1.76 mm	**Obv:** Susanna Blunt, Susan Taylor **Rev:** G.E. Kruger-Gray, Thomas Shingles	Smooth	Magnetic	↑↑

* Please Note: Due to market fluctuation the prices included in this chart are estimates only.

FIVE CENT DOUBLED DIE SUMMARY

It is not very common to come across doubled die examples on Canadian five cent coins from the 40s, 50s, 60s, and 70s. Even if found, these examples are usually in poor condition with the extra claw (DDR) varieties being the most prevalent.

Only a handful of dates have doubled die varieties on the obverse, which include the 2012 and 2013 five cent coins. To discover new examples over time, it is recommended to search through boxes from local banks.

Common Master Die Doubling Examples to Ignore

You may come across common (worthless) master die doubling on certain nickels from 1942, 1964, 1965, and 1966. If you're examining a 1942, 1964, 1965, or 1966 nickel, you might notice doubling on the stems of the left or right maple leaf on either side of the "5 CENTS" on the back of the coin.

However, if you're examining a 1964 nickel, you will find splitting on the tip of the "6" in the date. On the other hand, if you're examining a 2006 nickel, you will be able to spot extra claws in the center of the reverse.

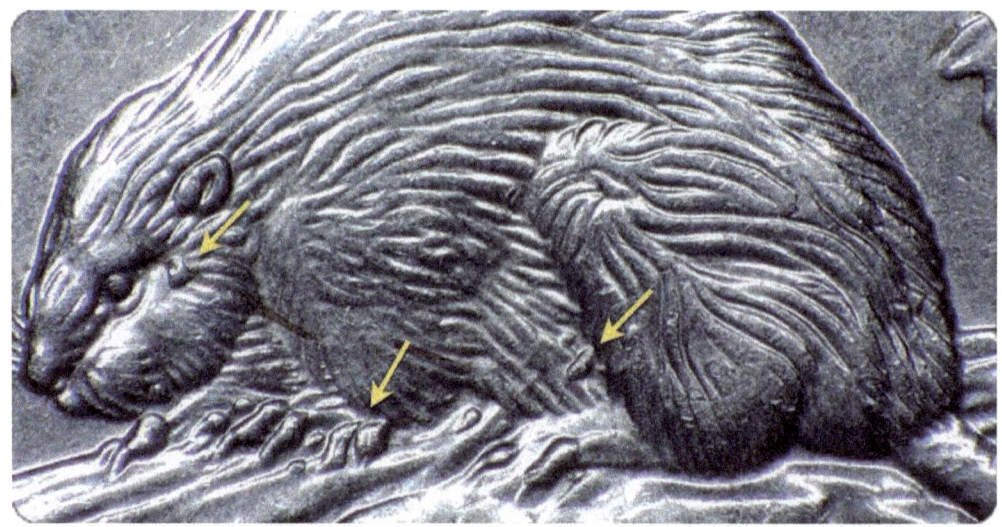

2006 5¢ featuring master die doubling

TEN CENT DOUBLED DIE LISTINGS

— Charts for the ten cent doubled die listings include mintages, designers and engravers information, compositions, weight, and previously sold prices when applicable. If no prices have been established yet they will be left blank (—). Prices included should be treated as estimates only and are in Canadian currency (CAD).

Doubled Die Reverse (DDR) - Examination Areas:

Finding doubled die examples on 10 cent coins is not as simple as other denominations due to their overall size. However, when doubled design details are found on the reverse of a 10 cent coin, they are usually located in the following areas.

- **CANADA** - Can show notching on the bottom of each letter.
- **10 CENTS** - Visible notching or splitting on the numbers and letters.
- **ROPES** - The ropes located on the bluenose can be completely doubled.
- **DATE** - Notching or splitting on the tips of each digit (2009 is master die doubling).
- **H** - Single designer initial can be completely doubled, or only feature notching.

Doubled Die Obverse (DDO) - Examination Areas:

Doubled die obverse examples on 10 cent coins will show visible split serifs or notching can be found on one letter, or all of the letters in the following obverse legends.

- **GEORGIVS VI - D:G: - REX - ET - IND:IMP:** - From 1937 to 1947.
- **GEORGIVS VI - DEI - GRATIA - REX** - From 1948 to 1952.
- **ELIZABETH II - D.G. REGINA** - From 1952 to 2022.

Doubled die varieties on the Canadian 10 cent coins are not very common, most of the examples that have been found are on key dates, semi key dates, or recently discovered.

Currently to date, there are only a handful of doubled die varieties for the Canadian 10 cent dimes from 1951 to 2012, further studying and searching of this denomination would likely produce more examples and new discoveries over time.

One thing to note when searching for doubled die varieties on all denominations, regardless of its size if present, a doubled die is in fact a genuine mint made variety.

1951 - GEORGIVS VI - 10¢ - DDR - TYPE 1

The 1951 Doubled Die Reverse Type 1 example shown here was won in an online auction and photographed by John O'Connor in 2023.

EXAMINATION NOTES:

51-VI-10C-DDR-T1

The 1951 doubled die reverse 10 Cent example shown here is an impressive variety that shows clear splitting and notching most visible on the reverse legend 10 CENTS.

Finding examples of this doubled die in any grade higher than AU has become scarce with a very low mintage and considered to some as a semi-key date.

Doubled numbers in the date can also be visible with minor notching in the bottom tip of the 1 and 9 and the inner loop of the 5.

1951 Georgivs VI - Doubled Die Reverse - Type 1							
DATE	EF-40	AU-50	MS-60	MS-62	MS-63	MS-64	MS-65
1951 VI - Normal Obv.	3.50	5.00	11.00	14.40	17.60	35.00	165.00
51-VI-10C-DDR-T1	15.00	22.00	51.50	64.00	155.00	280.00	670.00
Mintage	15,079,265						
Contents:	Weight:	Dimensions:	Engravers & Designers:		Edge/Rim:	Magnetism:	Die Axis:
80% Silver 20% Copper	2.33 Grams	18.03 mm x 1.16 mm	Obv: T.H. Paget Rev: Emanuel Hann		Reeded	Non-magnetic	↑↑

* Please Note: Due to market fluctuation the prices included in this chart are estimates only.

1951 - GEORGIVS VI - 10¢ - DDR - TYPE 2

The 1951 Doubled Die Reverse Type 2 example shown here was found and photographed by Jakob Miller while helping a friend sort through a Georgivs VI collection to determine values in 2023.

EXAMINATION NOTES:

51-VI-10C-DDR-T2

The 1951 doubled die reverse 10 Cent Type 2 example shown here is just as impressive as the Type 1, showing clear splitting and notching most visible on the reverse legend 10 CENTS.

Although both types being equally scarce, the Type 2 is much harder to find and has been eluding collectors for over 50 years.

A spread between the first hubbing impression and the second hubbing impression can also be found on the digits in the date.

1951 Georgivs VI - Doubled Die Reverse - Type 2						
DATE	EF-40	AU-50	MS-60	MS-62	MS-63	MS-64	MS-65
1951 VI - Normal Obv.	3.50	5.00	11.00	14.40	17.60	35.00	165.00
51-VI-10C-DDR-T2	15.00	22.00	51.50	64.00	155.00	280.00	670.00
Mintage	15,079,265						
Contents:	Weight:	Dimensions:	Engravers & Designers:	Edge/Rim:	Magnetism:	Die Axis:
80% Silver 20% Copper	2.33 Grams	18.03 mm x 1.16 mm	Obv: T.H. Paget Rev: Emanuel Hann	Reeded	Non-magnetic	↑↑

* Please Note: Due to market fluctuation the prices included in this chart are estimates only.

1952 - GEORGIVS VI - 10¢ - DDR

The 1952 Doubled Die Reverse example shown here was found and photographed by Roger Paulen in 2023.

EXAMINATION NOTES:

52-VI-10C-DDR

The 1952 doubled die reverse shown here was found and photographed by Roger Paulen in 2023 while examining the reverse side of the coin.

This doubled die reverse example may possibly be a new discovery as there are no available resources, or examples known for a doubled die on this date and denomination.

Clear notching can be seen on the digits in the date, and doubled letters can also be found the the legends CANADA and 10 Cents.

1952 Georgivs VI - Doubled Die Reverse							
DATE	EF-40	AU-50	MS-60	MS-62	MS-63	MS-64	MS-65
1952 VI - Normal Obv.	4.50	6.00	10.00	14.50	16.00	30.00	84.00
52-VI-10C-DDR	—	—	—	—	—	—	—
Mintage	10,474,455						
Contents:	Weight:	Dimensions:	Engravers & Designers:		Edge/Rim:	Magnetism:	Die Axis:
80% Silver 20% Copper	2.33 Grams	18.03 mm x 1.16 mm	**Obv:** T.H. Paget **Rev:** Emanuel Hann		Reeded	Non-magnetic	↑↑

* Please Note: Due to market fluctuation the prices included in this chart are estimates only.

1955 - ELIZABETH II - 10¢ - DDO

The 1955 Doubled Die Obverse example shown here was purchased on the internet and photographed by John O'Connor in 2023.

EXAMINATION NOTES:

55-QEII-10C-DDO

The 1955 Doubled Die Obverse is presumably the only example currently known, for now.

Splitting on the tips of the ribbons in the Queen's hair and the following letters in the obverse legends.

- "**E**" in ELIZABETH, DEI & REGINA
- "**L**" in ELIZABETH
- "**I**" in ELIZABETH, II, DEI & REGINA
- "**Z**" in ELIZABETH
- "**A**" in ELIZABETH
- "**B**" in ELIZABETH
- "**T**" in ELIZABETH
- "**H**" in ELIZABETH

1955 Elizabeth II - Doubled Die Obverse							
DATE	EF-40	AU-50	MS-60	MS-62	MS-63	MS-64	MS-65
1955 QEII - Normal Obv.	4.00	8.50	12.00	14.00	18.00	26.00	75.00
55-QEII-10C-DDO	—	—	—	—	—	—	—
Mintage	12,237,294						
Contents:	Weight:	Dimensions:	Engravers & Designers:		Edge/Rim:	Magnetism:	Die Axis:
80% Silver 20% Copper	2.33 Grams	18.03 mm x 1.16 mm	**Obv:** Mary Gillick, Thomas Shingles **Rev:** Emanuel Hann		Reeded	Non-magnetic	↑↑

* Please Note: Due to market fluctuation the prices included in this chart are estimates only.

1968 - ELIZABETH II - 10¢ - DDO

The 1968 Doubled Die Obverse example shown here was discovered and photographed by Roger Paulen in 2022, originally purchased as an error coin featuring an impressive obverse grease strike.

EXAMINATION NOTES:

68-QEII-10C-DDO

The doubled die was discovered and photographed by Roger Paulen in late 2022, it was originally purchased as a MS-60 Error dime featuring a large grease strike found on the obverse.

It also features a gap separating the first hubbing impression from the second misaligned hubbing impression seen on the letters of the obverse legend REGINA.

This 1968 doubled die has been struck on a nickel planchet at the Philadelphia mint when the United States was striking dimes for Canada in 1968.

1968 Queen Elizabeth II - Doubled Die Obverse							
DATE	EF-40	AU-50	MS-60	MS-62	MS-63	MS-64	MS-65
1968 QEII - Normal Obv.	10.00	24.50	32.00	38.00	40.00	65.00	120.00
68-QEII-10C-DDO	—	—	—	—	—	—	—
Mintage	85,170,000 (this mintage is only for the Philadelphia US Mint, not for the RCM)						
Contents:	Weight:	Dimensions:	Engravers & Designers:		Edge/Rim:	Magnetism:	Die Axis:
100% Nickel	2.07 Grams	18.03 mm x 1.16 mm	**Obv:** Arnold Machin **Rev:** Emanuel Hahn, Myron Cook		Reeded	Magnetic	↑↑

* Please Note: Due to market fluctuation the prices included in this chart are estimates only.

1973 - ELIZABETH II - 10¢ - DDO

The 1973 Doubled Die Obverse example shown here was discovered and photographed by John O'Connor in 2020 while searching circulated bank rolls in Kawartha Lakes, Ontario.

EXAMINATION NOTES:

73-QEII-10C-DDO

Although seemingly minor, the 1973 doubled die obverse features splitting and a small gap between the first and second hubbing impressions on the obverse legend REGINA.

Letters that features splitting or notching.

- "**R**" in REGINA
- "**E**" in REGINA
- "**G**" in REGINA
- "**I**" in REGINA
- "**N**" in REGINA
- "**A**" in REGINA

1973 Queen Elizabeth II - Doubled Die Obverse								
DATE	EF-40	AU-50	MS-60	MS-62	MS-63	MS-64	MS-65
1973 QEII - Normal Obv.	0.25	1.50	4.50	8.00	12.00	16.00	30.00
73-QEII-10C-DDO-T1	—	—	—	—	—	—	—
Mintage	167,715,435						
Contents:	Weight:	Dimensions:	Engravers & Designers:		Edge/Rim:	Magnetism:	Die Axis:
100% Nickel	2.07 Grams	18.03 mm x 1.16 mm	**Obv:** Arnold Machin, Myron Cook **Rev:** Emanuel Hahn, Myron Cook		Reeded	Magnetic	↑↑

*Please Note: Due to market fluctuation the prices included in this chart are estimates only.

1974 - ELIZABETH II - 10¢ - DDR - TYPE 2

The 1974 Doubled Die Reverse Type 2 example shown here was found and photographed by John O'Connor in 2020 while searching circulated bank rolls in Kawartha Lakes, Ontario.

EXAMINATION NOTES:

74-QEII-10C-DDR-T2

Unfortunately for this 1974 ten cent doubled die reverse suffered obvious signs of post mint damage, however there are distinctive doubled die features that are present. The legend 10 CENTS can be found with clear notching and splitting on the tips of each letter and the digits.

Visible in front of the bluenose, the designer initial H can be found with a completely separated second letter H directly behind it. There are minor doubled features on the latter ropes of the bluenose that can be found near the centre of the reverse.

1974 Queen Elizabeth II - Doubled Die Reverse - Type 2								
DATE	EF-40	AU-50	MS-60	MS-62	MS-63	MS-64	MS-65
1974 QEII - Normal Rev.	0.45	2.50	5.00	7.50	11.50	16.00	40.00
74-QEII-10C-DDR-T2	—	—	—	—	—	—	—
Mintage	201,566,565						
Contents:	Weight:	Dimensions:	Engravers & Designers:	Edge/Rim:	Magnetism:	Die Axis:	
100% Nickel	2.07 Grams	18.03 mm x 1.16 mm	**Obv:** Arnold Machin, Myron Cook **Rev:** Emanuel Hahn, Myron Cook	Reeded	Magnetic	↑↑	

*Please Note: Due to market fluctuation the prices included in this chart are estimates only.

2005-P - ELIZABETH II - 10¢ - DDR

The 2005-P Doubled Die Reverse example shown here was discovered and photographed by John O'Connor in 2020 while searching circulated bank rolls in Kawartha Lakes, Ontario.

EXAMINATION NOTES:

05P-QEII-10C-DDR

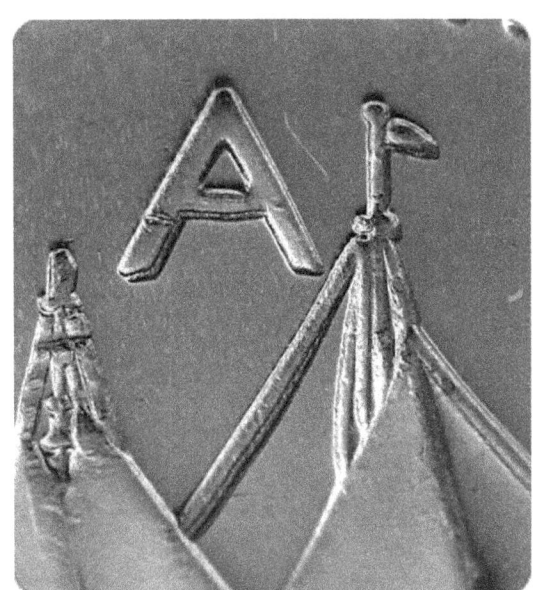

Although subtle, this 2005-P ten cent example features a minor gap and splitting between the first and second hubbing impression. Visible splitting with notching below the letters in CANADA and the rope below the second A.

The 2005-P doubled die obverse is an impressive and relatively scarce variety for modern Canadian dimes as it's discovery laid dormant for 15 years.

Magnification for this example should be in the 20x to 50x range to fully appreciate this new discovery.

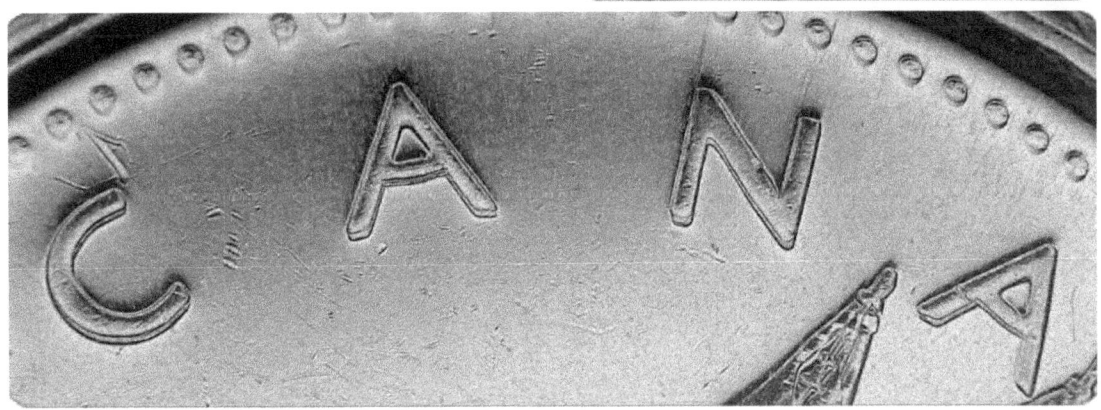

2005-P Queen Elizabeth II - Doubled Die Reverse							
DATE	EF-40	AU-50	MS-60	MS-62	MS-63	MS-64	MS-65
2005-P QEII - Normal Obv.	0.50	0.75	1.00	2.50	4.00	10.50	22.00
05P-QEII-10C-DDR	—	—	—	—	—	—	—
Mintage	211,350,000						
Contents:	Weight:	Dimensions:	Engravers & Designers:		Edge/Rim:	Magnetism:	Die Axis:
92% Steel, 5.5% Copper, 2.5% Nickel	1.75 Grams	18.03 mm x 1.22 mm	Obv: Susana Blunt, Susan Taylor Rev: Emanuel Hahn		Reeded	Magnetic	↑↑

* Please Note: Due to market fluctuation the prices included in this chart are estimates only.

2012 - ELIZABETH II - 10¢ - DDO - TYPE 1

The 2012 Doubled Die Obverse Type 1 example shown here was discovered and photographed by John O'Connor in 2020 while searching circulated bank rolls in Kawartha Lakes, Ontario.

EXAMINATION NOTES:

12-QEII-10C-DDO-T1

The 2012 Doubled Die Obverse Type 1 shown here has visible splitting of the first and second hubbing impressions.

Letters that can be found in the the obverse legend that features splitting or notching.

- "**R**" in REGINA
- "**E**" in REGINA
- "**G**" in REGINA
- "**I**" in REGINA
- "**N**" in REGINA
- "**A**" in REGINA

2012 Queen Elizabeth II - Doubled Die Obverse - Type 1								
DATE	EF-40	AU-50	MS-60	MS-62	MS-63	MS-64	MS-65	
2012 - QEII - Normal Obv.	0.50	0.75	2.00	2.50	4.00	8.50	18.00	
12-QEII-10C-DDO-T1	—	—	—	—	—	—	—	
Mintage	334,675,000							
Contents:	Weight:	Dimensions:	Engravers & Designers:		Edge/Rim:	Magnetism:	Die Axis:	
92% Steel, 5.5% Copper, 2.5% Nickel	1.75 Grams	18.03 mm x 1.22 mm	**Obv:** Susana Blunt, Susan Taylor **Rev:** Emanuel Hahn		Reeded	Magnetic	↑↑	

*Please Note: Due to market fluctuation the prices included in this chart are estimates only.

2012 - ELIZABETH II - 10¢ - DDO - TYPE 2

The 2012 Doubled Die Obverse Type 2 example shown here was discovered and photographed by John O'Connor in 2020 while searching circulated bank rolls in Kawartha Lakes, Ontario.

EXAMINATION NOTES:

12-QEII-10C-DDO-T2

The 2012 Doubled Die Obverse Type 2 shown here has visible splitting of the first and second hubbing impressions. Letters in the obverse legends that feature splitting or notching are shown below.

- "**E**" in ELIZABETH, DEI & REGINA
- "**T**" in ELIZABETH
- "**R**" in REGINA
- "**G**" in REGINA
- "**I**" in REGINA
- "**N**" in REGINA
- "**A**" in REGINA

2012 Queen Elizabeth II - Doubled Die Obverse - Type 2							
DATE	EF-40	AU-50	MS-60	MS-62	MS-63	MS-64	MS-65
2012 - QEII - Normal Obv.	0.50	0.75	2.00	2.50	4.00	8.50	18.00
12-QEII-10C-DDO-T2	—	—	—	—	—	—	—
Mintage	334,675,000						
Contents:	Weight:	Dimensions:	Engravers & Designers:		Edge/Rim:	Magnetism:	Die Axis:
92% Steel, 5.5% Copper, 2.5% Nickel	1.75 Grams	18.03 mm x 1.22 mm	**Obv:** Susana Blunt, Susan Taylor **Rev:** Emanuel Hahn		Reeded	Magnetic	↑↑

*Please Note: Due to market fluctuation the prices included in this chart are estimates only.

2012 - ELIZABETH II - 10¢ - DDR - TYPE 1

The 2012 Doubled Die Reverse Type 1 example shown here was discovered and photographed by John O'Connor in 2020 while searching circulated bank rolls in Kawartha Lakes, Ontario.

EXAMINATION NOTES:

12-QEII-10C-DDR-T1

Shown here, is the 2012 doubled die reverse 10 Cent example referred to as Type 1 that features a minor separation between the first and the second hubbing impression.

The first hubbing impression is most visible on the bottom of the numbers in the date 2012 and on the bottom of the numbers and letters found in the legend 10 CENTS.

This example is harder to find due to the weak separation, however the use of a USB microscope should be able to provide enough magnification.

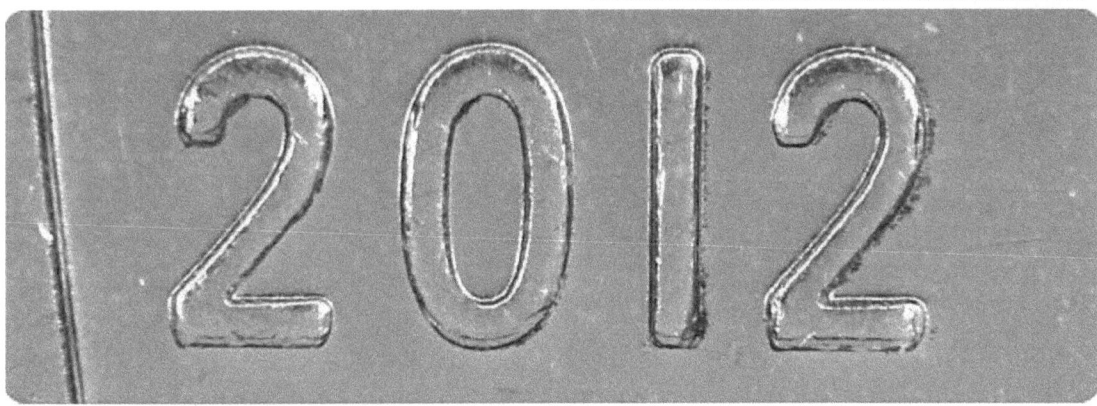

2012 Queen Elizabeth II - Doubled Die Reverse - Type 1							
DATE	EF-40	AU-50	MS-60	MS-62	MS-63	MS-64	MS-65
2012 - QEII - Normal Obv.	0.50	0.75	2.00	2.50	4.00	8.50	18.00
12-QEII-10C-DDR-T1	—	—	—	—	—	—	—
Mintage	334,675,000						
Contents:	Weight:	Dimensions:	Engravers & Designers:		Edge/Rim:	Magnetism:	Die Axis:
92% Steel, 5.5% Copper, 2.5% Nickel	1.75 Grams	18.03 mm x 1.22 mm	**Obv:** Susana Blunt, Susan Taylor **Rev:** Emanuel Hahn		Reeded	Magnetic	↑↑

Please Note: Due to market fluctuation the prices included in this chart are estimates only.

2012 - ELIZABETH II - 10¢ - DDR - TYPE 2

The 2012 Doubled Die Reverse Type 2 example shown here was discovered and photographed by John O'Connor in 2020 while searching circulated bank rolls in Kawartha Lakes, Ontario.

EXAMINATION NOTES:

12-QEII-10C-DDR-T2

Shown here, is the 2012 doubled die reverse 10 cent example known as Type 2 that features a minor separation between the first and the second hubbing impression.

Similar to Type 1, however the Type 2 shown here features a wider separation between the two hubbing impressions that caused notching and splits most noticeable on the reverse legend 10 CENTS.

Distinctive splitting can be seen on the top of the 1 in 10 CENTS and extra thickness of the letters when compared to a normal 2012 dime.

2012 Queen Elizabeth II - Doubled Die Reverse - Type 2							
DATE	EF-40	AU-50	MS-60	MS-62	MS-63	MS-64	MS-65
2012 - QEII - Normal Obv.	0.50	0.75	2.00	2.50	4.00	8.50	18.00
12-QEII-10C-DDR-T2	—	—	—	—	—	—	—
Mintage	334,675,000						
Contents:	Weight:	Dimensions:	Engravers & Designers:		Edge/Rim:	Magnetism:	Die Axis:
92% Steel, 5.5% Copper, 2.5% Nickel	1.75 Grams	18.03 mm x 1.22 mm	**Obv:** Susana Blunt, Susan Taylor **Rev:** Emanuel Hahn		Reeded	Magnetic	↑↑

*Please Note: Due to market fluctuation the prices included in this chart are estimates only.

TEN CENT DOUBLED DIE SUMMARY

The ten cent denomination may be small, but it has some impressive doubled die varieties with distinctive gaps between the first and second hubbing impressions. It's worth noting that BU examples of a doubled die on the ten cent coins, especially Georgivs VI examples, can sometimes carry a fair premium.

Don't overlook details on the bluenose such as the ropes, sail, and mast, especially the designer initial "H" found in front of the bluenose. These locations will show remnant of the first and second hubbing impression if a doubled die reverse is present.

Non-doubled Varieties Worth Noting

The 1968 ten cent coins were struck at two different locations in order to alleviate a shortage of coins at the time, 87,412,930 dimes were struck at the Royal Canadian Mint in Ottawa, while 85,170,000 dimes were struck at the Philadelphia Mint in the United States.

When trying to tell the difference between the RCM minted and Philly minted 1968 dimes, looking at the reeded edge will show two different types of reeds, for the Philly minted dimes the reeded edges are flat and not sharp, while the RCM dimes have sharp and pointed reeded edges.

Keeping in mind that condition plays a big part of being able to correctly identify this variety, if circulation flattens down the reeds over time it will make it difficult to tell the difference, this is why using uncirculated examples to compare with are beneficial.

Coins and Canada has a good comparison of the two varieties that can be found by clicking the link below, or doing a search on their website.

https://www.coinsandcanada.com/coins-prices.php?coin=10-cents-1968&years=10-cents-1965-1989

ONE DOLLAR DOUBLED DIE LISTINGS

— Charts for the one dollar doubled die listings include mintages, designers and engravers information, compositions, weight, and previously sold prices when applicable. If no prices have been established yet they will be left blank (—). Prices included should be treated as estimates only and are in Canadian currency (CAD).

Doubled Die Reverse (DDR) - Examination Areas:

For loon dollar examples and other reverse design varieties for the one dollar coin, the most common area to find doubled details are in the following locations.

- **CANADA** - Will usually show notching on the bottom of each letter.
- **DOLLAR** - Visible notching or splitting on the letters.
- **TREES** - Can feature doubled limbs.
- **RRC** - Designer initials can be completely doubled, or only feature notching.
- **ED** - Olympic loon designer initials can be completely doubled, or feature notching.
- **WATERLINES** - Only for the olympic loon dollars have been found doubled.
- **PROSPECTORS** - 2021 Klondike dollars only, both coloured and non-coloured.

Doubled Die Obverse (DDO) - Examination Areas:

When looking for a doubled die obverse examples on the Canadian 10 cent coins, split serifs and notching can be found on one letter, or all of the letters in the following obverse legends.

- **ELIZABETH II - D.G. REGINA** - Visible notching and splitting on the letters.
- **DATE** - Can show a minor to major spread between the doubled digits.
- **PORTRAIT** - portrait has been found to be doubled (most of the 2012 examples).

Searching for doubled die varieties on the Canadian 1 dollar coins are still producing relatively new discoveries on the obverse and the reverse designs. Continuing to search and examine this denomination over time will likely produce impressive examples of both obverse and reverse doubled die varieties.

2012 - ELIZABETH II - $1 - DDO - TYPE 1 - SECURITY

The 2012 Doubled Die Obverse Type 1 Security example shown here was found and photographed by John O'Connor in 2020 while searching circulated bank rolls in Kawartha Lakes, Ontario.

EXAMINATION NOTES:

12-QEII-1D-DDO-T1-SC

Identifying this doubled die obverse variety is fairly straight forward when looking at the date, notching is visible on the bottom top right side on both of the number 2's in the date 2012 and notching on the top right of the number 1.

Some examples of the 2012 loon dollars feature missing serifs on the top of the "I" in "REGINA" without doubled letters or numbers present, this die marker does not always mean it is a doubled die and the date should be carefully examined.

2012 Queen Elizabeth II - Doubled Die Obverse - Type 1 - Security							
DATE	EF-40	AU-50	MS-60	MS-62	MS-63	MS-64	MS-65
2012 - QEII - Normal Obv.	1.15	1.85	2.25	3.00	3.60	8.55	22.00
12-QEII-1D-DDO-T1-SC	—	—	—	—	—	—	—
Mintage	119,519,000						
Contents:	Weight:	Dimensions:	Engravers & Designers:		Edge/Rim:	Magnetism:	Die Axis:
91% Steel, 8.5% Brass	6.27 Grams	26.5 mm x 1.95 mm	**Obv:** Susana Blunt, Susan Taylor **Rev:** Robert R. Carmichael, T. Smith		Smooth	Magnetic	↑↑

*Please Note: Due to market fluctuation the prices included in this chart are estimates only.

2012 - ELIZABETH II - $1 - DDO - TYPE 2 - SECURITY

The 2012 Doubled Die Obverse Type 2 Security example shown here was found and photographed by John O'Connor in 2020 while searching circulated bank rolls in Kawartha Lakes, Ontario.

EXAMINATION NOTES:

12-QEII-1D-DDO-T2-SC

Visible separation and splitting on the bottom of the letters that make up ELIZABETH and on the top right side of the letters in D.G. REGINA. The first hubbing impression is visible on the right side of the date going Northeast.

2012 Queen Elizabeth II - Doubled Die Obverse - Type 2 - Security							
DATE	EF-40	AU-50	MS-60	MS-62	MS-63	MS-64	MS-65
2012 - QEII - Normal Obv.	1.15	1.85	2.25	3.00	3.60	8.55	22.00
12-QEII-1D-DDO-T2-SC	—	—	—	—	—	—	—
Mintage	119,519,000						
Contents:	Weight:	Dimensions:	Engravers & Designers:		Edge/Rim:	Magnetism:	Die Axis:
91% Steel, 8.5% Brass	6.27 Grams	26.5 mm x 1.95 mm	**Obv:** Susana Blunt, Susan Taylor **Rev:** Robert R. Carmichael, T. Smith		Smooth	Magnetic	↑↑

* Please Note: Due to market fluctuation the prices included in this chart are estimates only.

2012 - ELIZABETH II - $1 - DDO - TYPE 3 - SECURITY

The 2012 Doubled Die Obverse Type 3 Security example shown here was found and photographed by John O'Connor in 2020 while searching circulated bank rolls in Kawartha Lakes, Ontario.

EXAMINATION NOTES:

12-QEII-1D-DDO-T3-SC

Visible separation and splitting on the left side of the letters that make up ELIZABETH and on the bottom left side of the letters in D.G. REGINA. The first hubbing impression is visible on the lower left side of the date going Southwest.

2012 Queen Elizabeth II - Doubled Die Obverse - Type 3 - Security								
DATE	EF-40	AU-50	MS-60	MS-62	MS-63	MS-64	MS-65
2012 - QEII - Normal Obv.	1.15	1.85	2.25	3.00	3.60	8.55	22.00
12-QEII-1D-DDO-T3-SC	—	—	—	—	—	—	—
Mintage	119,519,000						
Contents:	Weight:	Dimensions:	Engravers & Designers:		Edge/Rim:	Magnetism:	Die Axis:
91% Steel, 8.5% Brass	6.27 Grams	26.5 mm x 1.95 mm	**Obv:** Susana Blunt, Susan Taylor **Rev:** Robert R. Carmichael, T. Smith		Smooth	Magnetic	↑↑
* Please Note: Due to market fluctuation the prices included in this chart are estimates only.							

2012 - ELIZABETH II - $1 - DDO - TYPE 4 - SECURITY

The 2012 Doubled Die Obverse Type 4 Security example shown here was found and photographed by John O'Connor in 2020 while searching circulated bank rolls in Kawartha Lakes, Ontario.

EXAMINATION NOTES:

12-QEII-1D-DDO-T4-SC

Visible separation and splitting on the right side of the letters that make up ELIZABETH and on the bottom left side of the letters in D.G. REGINA. The first hubbing impression is visible on the upper left side of the date going Northwest.

2012 Queen Elizabeth II - Doubled Die Obverse - Type 4 - Security							
DATE	EF-40	AU-50	MS-60	MS-62	MS-63	MS-64	MS-65
2012 - QEII - Normal Obv.	1.15	1.85	2.25	3.00	3.60	8.55	22.00
12-QEII-1D-DDO-T4-SC	—	—	—	—	—	—	—
Mintage	119,519,000						
Contents:	Weight:	Dimensions:	Engravers & Designers:		Edge/Rim:	Magnetism:	Die Axis:
91% Steel, 8.5% Brass	6.27 Grams	26.5 mm x 1.95 mm	**Obv:** Susana Blunt, Susan Taylor **Rev:** Robert R. Carmichael, T. Smith		Smooth	Magnetic	↑↑

* Please Note: Due to market fluctuation the prices included in this chart are estimates only.

2012 - ELIZABETH II - $1 - DDO - TYPE 5 - SECURITY

The 2012 Doubled Die Obverse Type 5 Security example shown here was found and photographed by John O'Connor in 2020 while searching circulated bank rolls in Kawartha Lakes, Ontario.

EXAMINATION NOTES:

12-QEII-1D-DDO-T5-SC

Visible separation and splitting on the right side of the letters that make up D.G. REGINA. The first hubbing impression is visible on the bottom of the numbers in the date going directly South.

2012 Queen Elizabeth II - Doubled Die Obverse - Type 5 - Security							
DATE	EF-40	AU-50	MS-60	MS-62	MS-63	MS-64	MS-65
2012 - QEII - Normal Obv.	1.15	1.85	2.25	3.00	3.60	8.55	22.00
12-QEII-1D-DDO-T5-SC	—	—	—	—	—	—	—
Mintage	119,519,000						
Contents:	Weight:	Dimensions:	Engravers & Designers:		Edge/Rim:	Magnetism:	Die Axis:
91% Steel, 8.5% Brass	6.27 Grams	26.5 mm x 1.95 mm	**Obv:** Susana Blunt, Susan Taylor **Rev:** Robert R. Carmichael, T. Smith		Smooth	Magnetic	↑↑
* Please Note: Due to market fluctuation the prices included in this chart are estimates only.							

2012 - ELIZABETH II - $1 - DDR - TYPE 1 - SECURITY

The 2012 Doubled Die Reverse Type 1 Security example shown here was found and photographed by John O'Connor in 2020 while searching circulated bank rolls in Kawartha Lakes, Ontario.

EXAMINATION NOTES:

12-QEII-1D-DDR-T1-SC

The 2012 loon dollars have two known doubled die reverse types. Shown here, is the Type 1 doubled die reverse variety that shows a minor separation of the first and second hubbing impression on the legend DOLLAR.

Notching can be found on the top left of each letter in the legend with visible remanence of the first hubbing impression.

Not easily seen with the naked eye, however using a loupe or USB microscope will make identifying this doubled die easier.

2012 Queen Elizabeth II - Doubled Die Reverse - Type 1 - Security							
DATE	EF-40	AU-50	MS-60	MS-62	MS-63	MS-64	MS-65
2012 - QEII - Normal Rev.	1.15	1.85	2.25	3.00	3.60	8.55	22.00
12-QEII-1D-DDR-T1-SC	—	—	—	—	—	—	—
Mintage	119,519,000						

Contents:	Weight:	Dimensions:	Engravers & Designers:	Edge/Rim:	Magnetism:	Die Axis:
91% Steel, 8.5% Brass	6.27 Grams	26.5 mm x 1.95 mm	**Obv:** Susana Blunt, Susan Taylor **Rev:** Robert R. Carmichael, T. Smith	Smooth	Magnetic	↑↑

* Please Note: Due to market fluctuation the prices included in this chart are estimates only.

2012 - ELIZABETH II - $1 - DDR - TYPE 2 - SECURITY

The 2012 Doubled Die Reverse Type 2 Security example shown here was found and photographed by John O'Connor in 2020 while searching circulated bank rolls in Kawartha Lakes, Ontario.

EXAMINATION NOTES:

12-QEII-1D-DDR-T2-SC

Unlike the 2012 Type 1 DDR, the Type 2 shown here has a larger spread separating the first and second hubbing impressions.

Similar to the Type 1 DDR, notching can be found on the top left and bottom right of each letter found in the reverse legend DOLLAR.

Finding this example in BU condition would be ideal as it will likely bring a fair premium due to this doubled die being a lot larger when compared to other 2012 examples that have been found.

2012 Queen Elizabeth II - Doubled Die Reverse - Type 2 - Security							
DATE	EF-40	AU-50	MS-60	MS-62	MS-63	MS-64	MS-65
2012 - QEII - Normal Rev.	1.15	1.85	2.25	3.00	3.60	8.55	22.00
12-QEII-1D-DDR-T2-SC	—	—	—	—	—	—	—
Mintage	119,519,000						
Contents:	Weight:	Dimensions:	Engravers & Designers:		Edge/Rim:	Magnetism:	Die Axis:
91% Steel, 8.5% Brass	6.27 Grams	26.5 mm x 1.95 mm	**Obv:** Susana Blunt, Susan Taylor **Rev:** Robert R. Carmichael, T. Smith		Smooth	Magnetic	↑↑

* Please Note: Due to market fluctuation the prices included in this chart are estimates only.

2012 - ELIZABETH II - $1 - DDO + DDR - TYPE 1 - SECURITY

The 2012 Security DDO + DDR example shown here was found and photographed by John O'Connor in 2020 while searching circulated bank rolls in Kawartha Lakes, Ontario.

EXAMINATION NOTES:

12-QEII-1D-DDO+DDR-T1-SC

Visible separation and splitting on the right side of the letters that make up ELIZABETH and on the left side of the letters in D.G. REGINA. Minor notching can also be visible on the top and bottom letters in CANADA.

2012 Queen Elizabeth II - Security - Doubled Die Obverse + Reverse								
DATE	EF-40	AU-50	MS-60	MS-62	MS-63	MS-64	MS-65	
2012 - QEII - Normal Obv.	1.15	1.85	2.25	3.00	3.60	8.55	22.00	
12-QEII-S-1D-DDO+DDR	—	—	—	—	—	—	—	
Mintage	119,519,000							
Contents:	Weight:	Dimensions:	Engravers & Designers:		Edge/Rim:	Magnetism:	Die Axis:	
91% Steel, 8.5% Brass	6.27 Grams	26.5 mm x 1.95 mm	**Obv:** Susana Blunt, Susan Taylor **Rev:** Robert R. Carmichael, T. Smith		Smooth	Magnetic	↑↑	

* Please Note: Due to market fluctuation the prices included in this chart are estimates only.

2012 - ELIZABETH II - $1 - DDO - OLYMPIC LOON

The 2012 Doubled Die Obverse Olympic Loon example shown here was found and photographed by John O'Connor in 2020 while searching circulated bank rolls in Kawartha Lakes, Ontario.

EXAMINATION NOTES:

12-QEII-1D-DDO-OL

The 2012 Olympic loon dollar, also referred to as the Lucky Loonie, can sometimes feature a doubled die obverse variety with a separation of the first and second hubbing impression that can be found on the letters that make up the obverse legend D.G. REGINA.

While examining the date on the 2012 Olympic Loon dollar, visible notching can also be found on the top right side of the number 1 and the top of the tails on both of the number 2's directly East.

	2012 Queen Elizabeth II - Doubled Die Obverse - Olympic Loon						
DATE	EF-40	AU-50	MS-60	MS-62	MS-63	MS-64	MS-65
2012 - QEII - Normal Obv.	1.50	2.00	3.50	4.00	5.00	0.50	30.00
12-QEII-1D-DDO-OL	—	—	—	—	—	—	—
Mintage	5,000,000						
Contents:	Weight:	Dimensions:		Engravers & Designers:		Edge/Rim:	Magnetism:	Die Axis:
91% Steel, 8.5% Brass	6.27 Grams	26.5 mm x 1.95 mm		**Obv:** Susana Blunt, Susan Taylor **Rev:** Emily Damstra, RCM		Smooth	Magnetic	↑↑

* Please Note: Due to market fluctuation the prices included in this chart are estimates only.

2012 - ELIZABETH II - $1 - DDO - GREY CUP

The 2012 Doubled Die Obverse Grey Cup example shown here was found and photographed by John O'Connor in 2020 while searching circulated bank rolls in Kawartha Lakes, Ontario.

EXAMINATION NOTES:

12-QEII-1D-DDO-GC

The 2012 Grey Cup dollar can sometimes be found featuring a nice doubled die obverse variety.

Clear separation between the first and the second hubbing impression can be found with notching affecting the obverse legend ELIZABETH II.

With a mintage of only 5 Million, finding an example of this doubled die in BU would be a great addition to any variety hunters personal collection as premiums will likely increase over time.

2012 Queen Elizabeth II - Doubled Die Obverse - Grey Cup							
DATE	EF-40	AU-50	MS-60	MS-62	MS-63	MS-64	MS-65
2012 - QEII - Normal Obv.	1.50	2.00	3.50	4.00	5.00	0.50	30.00
12-QEII-1D-DDO-GC	—	—	—	—	—	—	—
Mintage	5,000,000						
Contents:	Weight:	Dimensions:	Engravers & Designers:		Edge/Rim:	Magnetism:	Die Axis:
91% Steel, 8.5% Brass	6.27 Grams	26.5 mm x 1.95 mm	**Obv:** Susana Blunt, Susan Taylor **Rev:** Robert R. Carmichael, T. Smith		Smooth	Magnetic	↑↑

*Please Note: Due to market fluctuation the prices included in this chart are estimates only.

2014 - ELIZABETH II - $1 - DDR - OLYMPIC LOON

The 2014 Doubled Die Reverse Olympic Loon example shown here was found and photographed by John O'Connor in 2020 while searching circulated bank rolls in Kawartha Lakes, Ontario.

EXAMINATION NOTES:

14-QEII-1D-DDR-OL

The 2014 Olympic Loon, also referred to as the Lucky Loonie can sometimes be found featuring a doubled die reverse variety.

Visible separation between the first and the second hubbing impression can be found on the designer initials ED below the loons left wing.

There will be visible separation on the maple leaf, the 5 rings below the maple leaf, and the border around the Olympic Logo. Some minor splitting can also be found on the tips of the water ripples surrounding the loon.

Normal — Doubled

2014 Queen Elizabeth II - Doubled Die Reverse - Olympic Loon								
DATE	EF-40	AU-50	MS-60	MS-62	MS-63	MS-64	MS-65
2014 - QEII - Normal Obv.	1.50	2.00	3.50	4.00	5.00	0.50	30.00
14-QEII-1D-DDR-OL	—	—	—	—	—	—	—
Mintage	5,000,000						
Contents:	Weight:	Dimensions:	Engravers & Designers:	Edge/Rim:	Magnetism:	Die Axis:		
91% Steel, 8.5% Brass	6.27 Grams	26.5 mm x 1.95 mm	**Obv:** Susana Blunt, Susan Taylor **Rev:** Emily Damstra, RCM	Smooth	Magnetic	↑↑

* Please Note: Due to market fluctuation the prices included in this chart are estimates only.

2021 - ELIZABETH II - $1 - DDR -TYPE 1 - KLONDIKE NON COLOURED

The 2021 Doubled Die Reverse Type 1 Klondike Non Coloured example shown here was discovered and photographed by John O'Connor in 2022 while searching circulated bank rolls in Kawartha Lakes, Ontario.

EXAMINATION NOTES:

21-QEII-1D-DDR-T1-K-NC

The non coloured version of the 2021 Klondike dollar shown here was the first doubled die reverse variety that was found while searching circulated bank rolls and is referred to as Type 1.

Visible separation between the first and the second hubbing impression can be found on the back of the large prospector, as well as the top of his hat.

Separation is also visible on the back of smaller prospectors back, his hat, and behind his left foot. With a low mintage, BU examples could eventually see a fair premium.

2021 Queen Elizabeth II - Doubled Die Reverse - Type 1 - Klondike Non Coloured							
DATE	EF-40	AU-50	MS-60	MS-62	MS-63	MS-64	MS-65
2021 - QEII - Normal Rev.	1.00	1.50	2.25	3.00	3.55	8.75	24.00
21-QEII-DDR-T1-K-NC	—	—	—	—	—	—	—
Mintage	1,000,000						
Contents:	Weight:	Dimensions:	Engravers & Designers:		Edge/Rim:	Magnetism:	Die Axis:
91% Steel, 8.5% Brass	6.27 Grams	26.5 mm x 1.95 mm	**Obv:** RCM Staff **Rev Design:** Jori van der Linde.		Smooth	Magnetic	↑↑

* Please Note: Due to market fluctuation the prices included in this chart are estimates only.

2021 - ELIZABETH II - $1 - DDR -TYPE 2 - KLONDIKE NON COLOURED

The 2021 Doubled Die Reverse Type 2 Klondike Non Coloured example shown here was discovered and photographed by John O'Connor in 2022 while searching circulated bank rolls in Kawartha Lakes, Ontario.

EXAMINATION NOTES:

21-QEII-1D-DDR-T2-K-NC

The non coloured version of the 2021 Klondike dollar shown here was the second doubled die reverse variety that was found while searching circulated bank rolls and is referred to as Type 2.

Visible separation between the first and the second hubbing impression can be found on the front of the prospectors hat.

Separation is also visible on the front of smaller prospectors foot. With a low mintage of only 5 Million, BU examples could potentially see a fair premium in the future.

2021 Queen Elizabeth II - Doubled Die Reverse - Type 2 - Klondike Non Coloured							
DATE	EF-40	AU-50	MS-60	MS-62	MS-63	MS-64	MS-65
2021 - QEII - Normal Rev.	1.00	1.50	2.25	3.00	3.55	8.75	24.00
21-QEII-DDR-T2-K-NC	—	—	—	—	—	—	—
Mintage	1,000,000						
Contents:	Weight:	Dimensions:	Engravers & Designers:		Edge/Rim:	Magnetism:	Die Axis:
91% Steel, 8.5% Brass	6.27 Grams	26.5 mm x 1.95 mm	**Obv:** RCM Staff **Rev Design:** Jori van der Linde.		Smooth	Magnetic	↑↑

* Please Note: Due to market fluctuation the prices included in this chart are estimates only.

2021 - ELIZABETH II - $1 - DDR - KLONDIKE COLOURED

The 2021 Doubled Die Reverse Klondike Coloured example shown here was discovered and photographed by Jonny Gauvin in 2023.

EXAMINATION NOTES:

21-QEII-1D-DDR-K-C

The coloured version of the 2021 Klondike dollar shown here was the first doubled die reverse variety that was discovered by Jonny Gauvin.

Visible separation between the first and the second hubbing impression can be found on the front of the prospectors hat and his right hand.

Although similar to the 2021 non coloured version referred to as Type 2, the coloured version shown here was struck with a different working die. With a low mintage of only 5 Million, BU examples could potentially see a fair premium in the future.

2021 Queen Elizabeth II - Doubled Die Reverse - Type 1 - Klondike - Coloured								
DATE	EF-40	AU-50	MS-60	MS-62	MS-63	MS-64	MS-65
2021 - QEII - Normal Rev.	1.50	2.00	3.50	4.00	5.00	10.00	30.00
21-QEII-DDR-K-C	—	—	—	—	—	—	—
Mintage	2,000,000						
Contents:	Weight:	Dimensions:	Engravers & Designers:	Edge/Rim:	Magnetism:	Die Axis:
91% Steel, 8.5% Brass	6.27 Grams	26.5 mm x 1.95 mm	**Obv:** RCM Staff **Rev Design:** Jori van der Linde.	Smooth	Magnetic	↑↑

* Please Note: Due to market fluctuation the prices included in this chart are estimates only.

2022 - ELIZABETH II - $1 - DDR - SECURITY

The 2022 Doubled Die Reverse Security example shown here was discovered and photographed by John O'Connor in 2022 while searching circulated bank rolls in Kawartha Lakes, Ontario.

EXAMINATION NOTES:

22-QEII-1D-DDR-SC

The 2022 Loon Dollar doubled die reverse shown here features visible separation between the first and the second hubbing impression.

Although minor, when looking at the second last tree closest to the loons back, all four tree limbs on the right side of the tree will show small remanence of the first hubbing impression.

Due to no current (accurate) mintage report for this date and denomination there is no telling how common, or scarce this specific doubled die will be at this time.

2022 Queen Elizabeth II - Doubled Die Reverse - Security								
DATE	EF-40	AU-50	MS-60	MS-62	MS-63	MS-64	MS-65	
2022 - QEII - Normal Rev.	1.00	1.50	2.25	3.40	4.00	8.75	24.50	
22-QEII-1D-DDR-SC	—	—	—	—	—	—	—	
Mintage	Mintage Currently Unknown							
Contents:	Weight:	Dimensions:	Engravers & Designers:		Edge/Rim:	Magnetism:	Die Axis:	
91% Steel, 8.5% Brass	6.27 Grams	26.5 mm x 1.95 mm	**Obv:** RCM **Rev:** RCM		Smooth	Magnetic	↑↑	

* Please Note: Due to market fluctuation the prices included in this chart are estimates only.

ONE DOLLAR DOUBLED DIE SUMMARY

It is easier to find doubled die examples on one dollar coins compared to other denominations. This is not because they are less scarce, but due to their size and ease of examination. For over 50 years, one dollar coins have been widely searched for doubled die examples, from the 1945 silver dollars to the transition of the loon dollars in 1987. Most of Canada's known doubled die examples happen to be on the one dollar denomination.

Certain years for this denomination have an abundance of doubled die varieties, such as the 2012 and 2013 one dollar coins, which include the loon dollars, lucky loonies, hockey dollars, and other special edition dollars for 2012. While the loon dollars are still relatively common, they have produced some of the most impressive doubled die obverse and reverse varieties seen on Canadian coins.

If doubled die examples are found in BU condition, they will likely carry a fair premium in the future. Collectors and roll hunters should feel encouraged when searching rolls of Canadian one dollar coins, as almost every roll could possibly produce at least one doubled die example and possibly even a new discovery.

Possible Doubled Die Variety Worth Noting

If a doubled die obverse or reverse were to be found on the older style 2012 loon dollar that features the date on the reverse under the loon instead of below the Queen's portrait on the obverse, it would likely become more sought after compared to the other versions for 2012 that feature doubled dies.

Since it is a relatively scarce variety on its own with a low mintage of 2,414,00 if one was found with a doubled die on the obverse or the reverse, it would be two highly sought after varieties featured on a single coin. New collectors may also wonder why there were no dollar denominations struck for 1940 to 1944, this was due to the war efforts during that time.

TWO DOLLAR DOUBLED DIE LISTINGS

— Charts for the limited two dollar doubled die listings include mintages, designers and engravers information, compositions, weight, and previously sold prices when applicable. If no prices have been established yet they will be left blank (—). Prices included should be treated as estimates only and are in Canadian currency (CAD).

Doubled Die Reverse (DDR) - Examination Areas:

For the two dollar examples, the most common area to find doubled details on the reverse side of the coin are in the following locations.

- **CANADA** - Visible notching or splitting on the letters.
- **Number "2"** - The number 2 can sometimes feature notching.
- **DOLLARS** - Will usually show notching on the bottom of each letter.

Doubled Die Obverse (DDO) - Examination Areas:

When looking for a doubled die obverse examples on the Canadian 2 dollar coins, notching can be found on one letter, or all of the letters in the following obverse legends.

- **ELIZABETH II - D.G. REGINA** - Visible notching and splitting on the letters.
- **PORTRAIT** - portrait has been found to be doubled (most of the 2012 examples).

Finding or discovering new doubled die varieties on the Canadian 2 dollar coins has proven to be fairly difficult and still relatively new. There are not very many doubled die examples that have been found or discovered for this specific denomination since the mint started producing the 2 dollar coins in 1996.

So far, doubled die variety examples have only been found on the 2011, 2012, 2013 and 2021 two dollar coins. There are still numerous dates that can be searched and could potentially yield new discoveries over time.

2012 - ELIZABETH II - $2 - DDO - TYPE 1 - SECURITY

The 2021 Doubled Die Reverse Type 1 Security example shown here was found and photographed by John Wayne O'Connor in 2021 while searching circulated rolls in Kawartha Lakes, Ontario.

EXAMINATION NOTES:

12-QEII-2D-DDO-T1-SC

The 2012 doubled die obverse Type 1 security toonie shown here has notching found on the right side of the digits in the date 2012.

There are also remanence of notching found on the obverse legend REGINA most noticeable on the bottom left side of the letters.

Doubled die varieties being found or discovered on the 2012 two dollar coins are not all that common, mainly because collectors and roll hunters simply did not know they existed until recently.

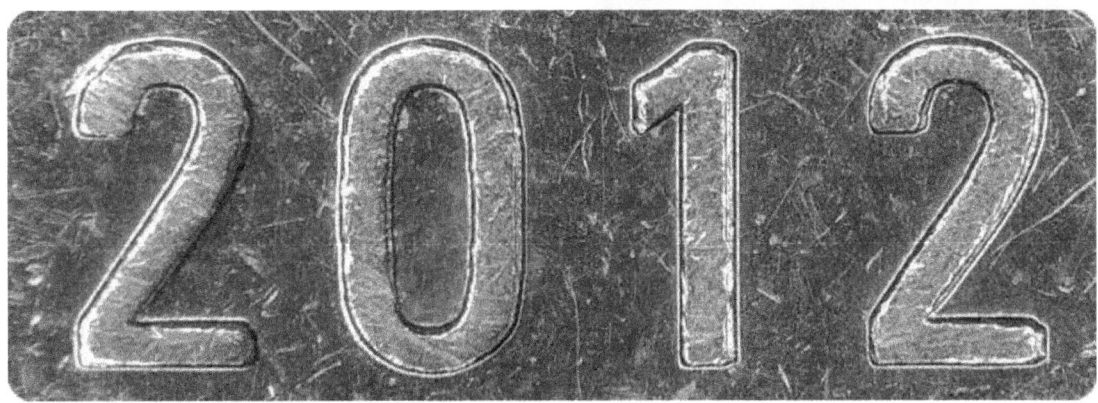

2012 Queen Elizabeth II - Doubled Die Obverse - Type 1 - Security							
DATE	EF-40	AU-50	MS-60	MS-62	MS-63	MS-64	MS-65
2012 - QEII - Normal Rev.	3.50	4.00	6.00	9.50	12.00	16.00	42.00
12-QEII-2D-DDO-T1-SC	—	—	—	—	—	—	—
Mintage	84,185,000						
Contents:	Weight:	Dimensions:	Engravers & Designers:		Edge/Rim:	Magnetism:	Die Axis:
91% Steel, 8.5% Brass	6.27 Grams	28 mm x 1.75 mm	Obv: Susana Blunt, Susan Taylor Rev: Robert R. Carmichael, T. Smith		Smooth	Magnetic	↑↑

* Please Note: Due to market fluctuation the prices included in this chart are estimates only.

2012 - ELIZABETH II - $2 - DDO - TYPE 2 - SECURITY

The 2021 Doubled Die Reverse Type 2 Security example shown here was found and photographed by John Wayne O'Connor in 2021 while searching circulated rolls in Kawartha Lakes, Ontario.

EXAMINATION NOTES:

12-QEII-2D-DDO-T2-SC

Although this 2012 doubled die obverse Type 2 security toonie is fairly circulated, it still features impressive notching on the bottom of the letters in the obverse legend ELIZABETH.

Notching can also be found on the bottom left side of the digits in the date 2012.

There are only a few known doubled die varieties for the obverse of the 2012 two dollar coins to date. Examining the obverse and the reverse of this date and denomination will likely produce more doubled die types like seen on the 2012 loon dollars.

2012 Queen Elizabeth II - Doubled Die Obverse - Type 2 - Security							
DATE	EF-40	AU-50	MS-60	MS-62	MS-63	MS-64	MS-65
2012 - QEII - Normal Rev.	3.50	4.00	6.00	9.50	12.00	16.00	42.00
12-QEII-2D-DDO-T2-SC	—	—	—	—	—	—	—
Mintage	84,185,000						
Contents:	Weight:	Dimensions:	Engravers & Designers:		Edge/Rim:	Magnetism:	Die Axis:
91% Steel, 8.5% Brass	6.27 Grams	28 mm x 1.75 mm	**Obv:** Susana Blunt, Susan Taylor **Rev:** Robert R. Carmichael, T. Smith		Smooth	Magnetic	↑↑

* Please Note: Due to market fluctuation the prices included in this chart are estimates only.

2012 - ELIZABETH II - $2 - DDO - HMS SHANNON

The 2012 HMS Shannon Doubled Die Obverse example shown here was discovered and photographed by Jonny Gauvin in 2022 while looking over examples from his 2 Dollar collection.

EXAMINATION NOTES:

12-QEII-2D-DDO-HMS

The 2012 HMS Shannon doubled die obverse features splitting on the digits in 2012 with minor notching present. Splitting can also be found on the left side of the maple lead with the date 1812 in the centre.

Searching more HMS Shannon $2 coins may produce more types of doubled die varieties on the obverse and possibly the reverse. Since there are an abundance of doubled die varieties for 2012 there are likely more types waiting to be discovered.

2012 Queen Elizabeth II - Doubled Die Obverse - HMS Shannon							
DATE	EF-40	AU-50	MS-60	MS-62	MS-63	MS-64	MS-65
2012 - QEII - Normal Rev.	3.50	4.00	6.00	9.50	12.00	16.00	30.00
12-QEII-2D-DDO-T1-HMS	—	—	—	—	—	—	—
Mintage	5,000,000						
Contents:	Weight:	Dimensions:		Engravers & Designers:	Edge/Rim:	Magnetism:	Die Axis:
91% Steel, 8.5% Brass	6.27 Grams	28 mm x 1.75 mm		Obv: Susana Blunt, Susan Taylor Rev: Robert R. Carmichael, T. Smith	Smooth	Magnetic	↑↑

* Please Note: Due to market fluctuation the prices included in this chart are estimates only.

TWO DOLLAR DOUBLED DIE SUMMARY

The search for doubled die examples on the two dollar coin is ongoing since this denomination only came into existence in 1996. Despite a handful of collectors and roll hunters sifting through rolls of two dollar coins for this specific variety type, only a few examples have been found so far.

It's impossible to determine the actual number of doubled die varieties until more collectors and roll hunters examine both sides of this denomination as it is still unclear how common or uncommon they are until more examples are found.

Non-doubled Varieties Worth Noting

A respectable variety worth noting is the 2010 and the 2019 toonies with 14 serrations and 16 serrations. Below is a photo of 14 serrations on the top, and 16 serrations on the bottom.

Finding examples to compare to in uncirculated condition are ideal, both the 2010 and the 2019 varieties carry a fair premium when found in UNC condition and are still relatively easy to find while roll hunting.

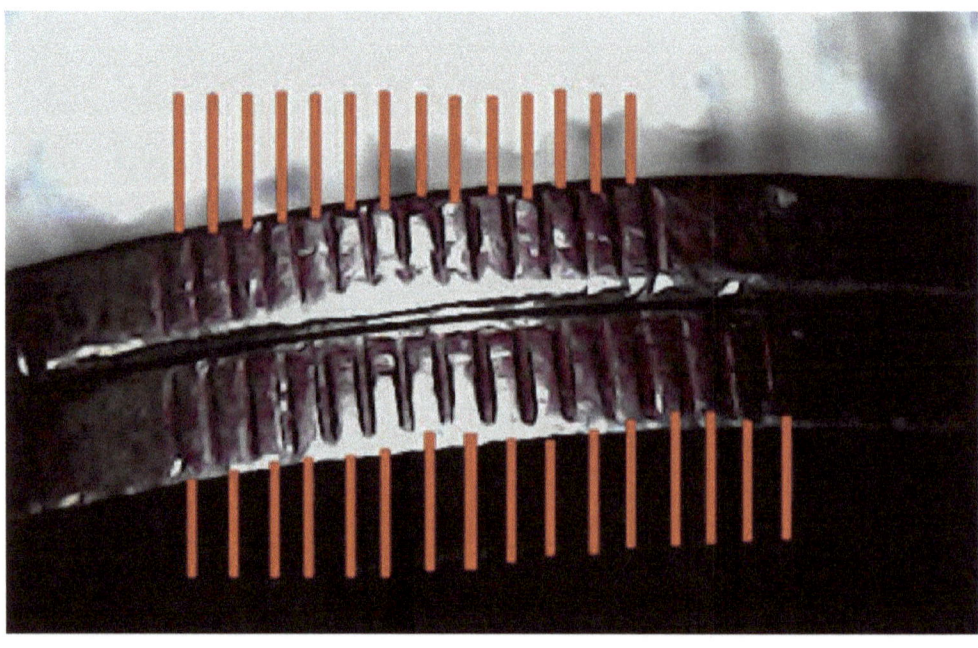

DOUBLED DIE REFERENCE LIST

Please note that the inclusion of usernames, websites, or first and last names in the reference list under the "**SOURCE/LINK**" sections does not imply personal responsibility for the discovery of the referenced doubled die variety.

The individuals mentioned in the reference list are experts, authors, long-time coin collectors, and well-established members of the Coin Community Forum who have given written permission to include direct links to their research and photographs related to the doubled die variety being referenced with full recognition of their work.

Clicking on a website, username, or full name under the "**SOURCE/LINK**" section of the reference list will redirect readers to a website, image/images, or a Coin Community Forum post. Please note that are are some non-clickable names, usernames, websites, or comments under the "**SOURCE/LINKS**" included.

Although re-punched die varieties are not technically doubled dies that happened during the process of creating the working dies, some re-punched varieties are included as they are still genuine doubled varieties that occurred after the hubbing of the working dies, with details such as last digits in the date that were hand-punched onto the surface of the finished working dies before any coins have been struck.

Please note that some listings from Coins and Canada in the reference list may not include a listing number, but they can be viewed on the first page of the date and denomination on their website by clicking the included link or visiting www.coinsandcanada.com and using the search bar for the date and variety.

REFERENCE LIST DISCLAIMER:

The author of Modern Canadian Doubled Die Varieties is not responsible for any third party advertisements, pop-ups, un-related subjects, or material that may be hosted on websites readers are directed to while clicking links found throughout the reference list.

All information that can be found in the reference list, including the information that has been provided by those who are listed in the special mentions found on the last page of Modern Canadian Doubled Die Varieties, must not be copied and are subject to individual copyright protections. Requesting written permission from each individual, author, expert, website moderator, or company must be correctly obtained.

1 CENT: 1941 - 2008

DATE	VARIETY	COMMENTS	SOURCE/LINK
1941	DDO-T1	All obverse legends doubled in a clock-wise direction - Doubled HP.	John O'Connor
1941	DDO-T2	Only the "S" in "GEORGIVS" is doubled, similar to DDO-T1 - Normal HP.	John O'Connor
1941	DDO-T3-HP	Obverse HP initials have been doubled.	John O'Connor
1949	DDO	Split serifs can be found on the letter "S" in the obverse legend "GEORGIVS".	John O'Connor
1949	RPD	Last 9 in the date shows a minor but obvious repunch visible on the tip and loop of the digit.	John O'Connor
1951	DDO-T1	Doubled obverse legends "GRATIA" and "REX" going in a clock-wise direction.	Reported by Alan Herbert to Ken Potter
1951	DDO-T2	Doubled obverse legends "GRATIA" and "DEI" going in a counter clock-wise direction.	John O'Connor
1957	DDO	Doubled obverse legend "ELIZABETH".	John O'Connor
1964	DDR-T1-BUD	Doubled bud going N/W of the main bud.	John O'Connor
1964	DDR-T2-BUD	Doubled bud going N/W of the main bud.	Coins and Canada #2619
1964	DDR-T3-SPINE	An extra (doubled) spine can be seen between the bud and the main spine.	John O'Connor
1964	DDR-T4-SPINE	An extra (doubled) spine can be seen protruding from the main bud.	John O'Connor
1964	DDR-T5-SPINE	A doubled spine between the bud and spine further from the crevice on the Reverse.	CCF: Fourmack
1964	DDR-T6-SPINE	Doubled spine can be seen attached to the bottom of the main bud and spine.	CCF: Fourmack
1964	DDR-T7-SPINE	Found under Zoell #R86n - Major coin varieties - Fourth Edition #1 - 1966 hosted on C.A.C.	Coins and Canada
1964	DDR-T8-SPINE	Doubled spine can be seen attached to the bottom of the bud with a slight bend.	Roger Paulen
1964	DDR-T9-SPINE	A doubled spine can be seen above the main spine in a north-east direction.	Roger Paulen
1965	DDR-BUD	A visible doubled bud protruding north-west on the top of the main bud.	Ken Potter

		1 CENT REFERENCES CONTINUED		
1966	DDR-T1-BUD	Small extra bud protruding from the right side of the main bud.	Coins and Canada #168
1966	DDR-T2-SPINE	Small extra spine visible on the right side of the bud.	Coins and Canada #761
1967	DDO	Becoming scarce in higher grades, showing doubled legends on the obverse.	John O'Connor
1968	DDR-SPINE	An extra spine visible on the left side of the bud.	Can be found searching the CCF
1969	DDR-BRANCH	Doubled branch N/W of the main bud.	Can be found searching the CCF
1970	DDR-BUD	Small visible doubled bud above the main bud on the reverse, discovered by Jo Vautor in 2012.	Joe Vautor
1972	DDR-T1-BUD	Doubled bud N/W of the main bud.	John O'Connor
1972	DDR-T2-BUD	Obvious doubled bud and branch N/W of the main bud and branch.	John O'Connor
1972	DDR-T3-SPINE	Small extra spine on the right side of the bud.	Coins and Canada #644
1974	DDR-SPINE	Extra spine visible on the right side of the bud.	Can be found searching the CCF
1975	DDO	Harder to find in higher grades. Full doubled legend on the Obverse.	Tanner Scott
1976	DDO-T1	Elusive and hard to find in any grade with full doubled obverse legends.	John O'Connor
1976	DDO-T2	Equally as elusive as V1 with doubled legends go in the opposite direction.	John O'Connor
1979	DDO	Doubled obverse legend ELIZABETH, with distinctive separation on the letter Z, and E.	CCF: Ondiwave
1985	DDR-BUD	Small extra bud protruding from the right side of the main bud.	Coins and Canada #1324
1993	DDR-SPINE	Extra spine protruding between the main spine and bud found on the reverse.	Coins and Canada #2452
1994	DDO-T1	Shows visible doubling in a clock-wise direction in the obverse legend D.G. REGINA.	John O'Connor
1994	DDO-T2	Doubling in a counter clock-wise direction in the obverse legend ELIZABETH II.	CCF: Numidan
2008	DDR	Doubled 8 visible on the top right of the digit.	John O'Connor

5 CENTS: 1947 - 2020

DATE	VARIETY	COMMENTS	SOURCE/LINK
1947	RPD	Reverse date shows a repunched 7, likely 3 separate times, common.	Common, might be Master Die Doubling
1947-ML	RPD	Reverse date shows a repunched 7, likely 3 separate times, common.	Common, might be Master Die Doubling
1955	DDR-CLW	Although minor, an extra claw right above the first claw can be seen.	Coins and Canada #3628
1957	DDR-CLW	Extra claw between the knuckles of the rear paw of the beaver found on the reverse.	Coins and Canada #3629
1958	DDR-CLW	Extra claw between the knuckles of the rear paw of the beaver found on the reverse.	Coins and Canada #2282
1960	DDR-T1-CLW	Extra claw can be seen above the claw on the rear paw in a N/W direction.	Tanner Scott
1960	DDR-T2-CLW	Extra claw can bee seen directly North above the claw on the rear paw.	Tanner Scott
1962	DDR-CLW	Extra claw between the knuckles of the rear paw of the beaver found on the reverse.	Coins and Canada #2276
1963	DDR-CLW	Remanence of an extra claw northwest below the beavers belly.	Tanner Scott
1964	DDR-CLW	Minor extra claw between the knuckles of the rear paw of the beaver found on the reverse.	John O'Connor
1965	DDR-T1-CLW	Extra claw above the two claws found on the rear paw of the beaver on the reverse.	John O'Connor
1965	DDR-T2-S5	Small 5 in the date found on the reverse.	John O'Connor
1965	DDR-T3-R5	Regular 5 in the date is doubled with notching.	John O'Connor
1966	DDR-T1-CLW	Extra claw found in front of the beavers rear paw under the belly on the reverse.	John O'Connor
1966	DDR-T2-CLW	Identical to DDR-T1-CLW but without the die chips in the loops of the 6's in the date.	John O'Connor
1968	DDR-CLW	Extra claw can be seen directly West of the claw on the rear paw.	Tanner Scott
1972	DDR-T1-CLW	Extra claw found in front of the rear paw under the belly of the beaver found on the reverse.	John O'Connor

		5 CENT REFERENCES CONTINUED		
1972	DDR-T2-CLW	Extra claw between the knuckles of the rear paw of the beaver found on the reverse.	Coins and Canada #3691
1978	DDR-CLW	Although minor, an extra thin claw is visible underneath the first claw on the rear beaver paw.	Coins and Canada #4173
1979	DDR-CLW	Extra claw directly above the first claw on the rear paw.	Tanner Scott
1980	DDR-CLW	Extra claw between the two claws found on the rear paw of the beaver.	Coins and Canada #3992
1984	DDR-CLW	Extra claw between the two rear claws on the beavers rear paw, identical to 1986 Extra Claw.	John O'Connor
1985	DDR-CLW	Extra claw between the two rear claws on the beavers rear paw, similar to the 1986 extra claw.	Confirmed on a Social Media Post
1986	DDR-CLW	Extra claw between the knuckles of the rear paw of the beaver found on the reverse.	Tanner Scott
1988	DDR-CLW	Similar to the 1984 and 1986 extra claw DDR.	Coins and Canada #3663
1990	DDR-CLW	Extra claw between the knuckles of the rear paw of the beaver found on the reverse.	Coins and Canada #3700
1993	DDR-CLW	Extra claw between the knuckles of the rear paw of the beaver found on the reverse.	Coins and Canada #3993
2007	DDR-CLW	Extra claw between the knuckles of the rear paw of the beaver found on the reverse.	Coins and Canada #3988
2008	DDR-CLW	Extra claw right above the first claw on the rear paw of the beaver found on the reverse.	Coins and Canada #2289
2011	DDR-CLW	Extra claw right above the second claw on the rear paw of the beaver found on the reverse.	Coins and Canada #1292
2012	DDO	Doubled legend "ELIZABETH II" on the obverse.	John O'Connor
2012	DDR-CLW	Extra claw right beside last claw on rear paw.	John O'Connor
2013	DDR-CLW	Extra claw between the knuckles of the rear paw of the beaver found on the reverse.	Coins and Canada #4160
2013	DDO-T1	Most visible on the obverse legends, compare with provided photos.	John O'Connor
2013	DDO-T2	Most visible on the obverse legends, compare with provided photos.	John O'Connor
2013	DDO-T3	Most visible on the obverse legends, compare with provided photos.	John O'Connor

	5 CENT REFERENCES CONTINUED			
2013	DDO-T4	Most visible on the obverse legends, compare with provided photos.		John O'Connor
2016	DDR	Doubled front and rear paws directly underneath each other.		John O'Connor
2020	DDR	Doubled front and rear paws directly underneath each other, similar to the 2016 DDR.		John O'Connor

10 CENTS: 1951 - 2012

DATE	VARIETY	COMMENTS	SOURCE/LINK
1951	DDR-T1	Doubled "10 Cents" and "1951" with noticeable notching and split serifs.	John O'Connor
1951	DDR-T2	Doubled "10 Cents" and "1951" with notching and splits in a different direction compared to T1.	Jakob Miller
1952	DDR	Doubled 1952 with nice separation.	Roger Paulen
1955	DDO	Doubled letters in ELIZABETH II + Ribbon.	John O'Connor
1968	DDO	Doubled obverse legends going counter-clockwise.	Roger Paulen
1973	DDO	Doubled letters most noticeable on "REGINA" on the obverse.	John O'Connor
1974	DDR-T1	Doubled Date, 10 Cents & H found on the reverse, see provided photos.	John O'Connor
1974	DDR+DDO-T1	Doubled Date, 10 Cents & H found on the reverse and in "REGINA" found on the obverse.	Can be found searching the CCF
1975	DDO	Doubled letters most noticeable on "REGINA" on the obverse, scarce.	Was available on eBay in 2021.
2005-P	DDR	Doubled Canada, Date, Top Sail Lines, H & 10 Cents on the reverse.	John-O'Connor
2012	DDO-T1	Most visible on the obverse legends, compare with provided photos.	John O'Connor
2012	DDO-T2	Most visible on the obverse legends, compare with provided photos.	John O'Connor
2012	DDR-T1	Most visible on the date and 10 CENTS, compare with provided photos.	John O'Connor
2012	DDR-T2	Most visible on the date and 10 CENTS, compare with provided photos.	John O'Connor

REFERENCE LIST   PAGE 147

25 CENTS: 1953 - 1972

DATE	VARIETY	COMMENTS	SOURCE/LINK
1953	DDR	Doubled 53 in the date on the reverse.	Coins and Canada #2336
1955	DDR	Doubled 55 in the date on the reverse.	Coins and Canada #1533
1972	DDR-T1	Doubled "H" Designer Initial. VCR#1/DDR#1	Ken Potter
1972	DDR-T2	Doubled "H" Designer Initial and CANADA. VCR#2/DDR#2	Ken Potter

50 CENTS: 1943 - 1996

DATE	VARIETY	COMMENTS	SOURCE/LINK
1943	RPD	The 4 and 3 has been re-punched once, visible on the right hand side of the digits.	Jakob Miller
1945	VCR#2/ RPD#2	The 5 has been repunched once, visible on the top side of the digit.	Ken Potter
1947-C7	RPD	Repunched Curved 7 showing split serifs in the top right hand side of the 7 in the date.	Coins and Canada #477
1947-S7	RPD	Repunched Straight 7 showing notching in the top left hand side of the 7 in the date.	Coins and Canada #977
1951	DDO-T1	Doubled "DEI" can be found on the obverse similar to the DDO Type 2 small cent.	Jakob Miller
1951	DDO-T2	Doubled HP found below the portrait of Georgivs VI on the obverse.	Coins and Canada
1952	DDO	Doubled HP found below the portrait of Georgivs VI on the obverse.	Jakob Miller
LITTLE WILD ONES STERLING SILVER 50 CENT PROOF SET			
1996	Moose Calf DDR	Visible split serifs and separation found on "CANADA" the date "1996" as well as "50 CENTS" found on the reverse of all 4 coins from the 1996 Little Wild Ones 4 Coin Set. NOTE: The doubled die reverse is most noticeable on the Moose Calf coin. **These coins were not issued for circulation.**	John O'Connor
1996	Wood Ducklings DDR		
1996	Cougar Kittens DDR		
1996	Black Bear Cubs DDR		

1 DOLLAR: 1945 - 2022

DATE	VARIETY	COMMENTS	SOURCE/LINK
1945	DDR	Doubled 5 in the date on the reverse.	Coins and Canada #1765
1945	DDO-T1	Doubled "HP" below Georgivs VI on the obverse.	Coins and Canada
1945	DDO-T2	"HP" doubled up to 4 times below Georgivs VI on the obverse.	Coins and Canada
1946	DDO-T1	"HP" doubled up to 4 times below Georgivs VI on the obverse.	Coins and Canada
1946	DDO-T2	Doubled obverse portrait visible on the eye, ear and nose - HP Quadrupled. VCR#1/DDO#1	Ken Potter
1947-PNT	RPD	Repunched 4 in the date on the reverse.	Coins and Canada #3389
1947-PNT	DDO-T2	Doubled "HP" found below Georgivs VI on the obverse.	Coins and Canada #3417
1947-PNT	DDO-T3	"HP" Doubled up to 3 times below Georgivs VI on the obverse.	Coins and Canada
1947-PNT	DDO-T4	"HP" Doubled up to 4 times below Georgivs VI on the obverse.	Coins and Canada
1947-BLT	DDO-T5	Doubled "HP" below Georgivs VI on the obverse.	Coins and Canada
1947-BLT	DDR-T6	Doubled 7 in the date found on the reverse.	Coins and Canada
1947-L	DDO-T8	Doubled "HP" below Georgivs VI on the obverse.	Coins and Canada
1950	DDO-T1	Doubled "HP" below Georgivs VI on the obverse. **Arnprior**	Coins and Canada
1951	DDO	Doubled "HP" below Georgivs VI on the obverse. ** Full Water Lines**	Coins and Canada #1766
1952	DDO	Doubled "HP" below Georgivs VI on the obverse. ** Full Water Lines**	Coins and Canada #1676
1968	DDR-T1	Doubled water line in front of the canoe on the reverse.	Coins and Canada #4522

	1 DOLLAR REFERENCES CONTINUED			
1968	DDR-T2	Doubled 68 and "DOLLAR" on the reverse.	Coins and Canada #889
1968	DDR-T3	Reverse legend "DOLLAR" shows notching.	John O'Connor
1974	VCR#1/ DDR#1	Doubled north yoke directly above the main yoke left from the final hubbing impression, Type 1.	Ken Potter
1974	VCR#2/ DDR#2	Doubled north-west yoke directly above the main yoke left from the final hubbing impression.	Ken Potter
1974	VCR#3/ DDR#3	Doubled east yoke between the main yoke left from the final hubbing impression and the ox's head.	Ken Potter
1974	VCR#4/ DDR#4	Doubled smaller north yoke directly above the main yoke left from the final hubbing impression, Type 2.	Ken Potter
1974	VCR#5/ DDR#5	Doubled yoke wedged between the bottom of the lower roof and the inside loop of the O.	Ken Potter
1974	VCR#6/ DDR#6	Doubled design details visible between the bottom of the top roof, and the top of the lower roof.	Ken Potter
1974	VCR#7/ DDR#7	Doubled design details visible on the west edge of the lower roof.	Ken Potter
1974	VCR#8/ DDR#8	Visible impression of the top north-west edge on the bottom of the lower roof, Type 1	Ken Potter
1974	VCR#9/ DDR#9	Doubled north-west top edge of the lower roof, Type 1	Ken Potter
1974	VCR#10/ DDR#10	Doubled north-west top edge of the lower roof, Type 2	Ken Potter
1974	VCR#11/ DDR#11	Doubled design details visible between the yoke and ox's horn.	Ken Potter
1974	VCR#12/ DDR#12	Doubled design detail wedged between the top of the lower roof and the inside loop of the O.	Ken Potter
1974	VCR#13/ DDR#13	Doubled horizontal lines visible between the two buildings above the ox's shoulders.	Ken Potter
1974	VCR#14/ DDR#14	Visible impression of the top north-west edge on the bottom of the lower roof, Type 2	Ken Potter
1974	VCR#15/ DDR#15	Visible impression of the top north-west edge of the lower roof extending into the building.	Ken Potter

1 DOLLAR REFERENCES CONTINUED

1974	VCR#16/ DDR#16	Doubled west yoke directly beside the main yoke from the final hubbing impression.		Ken Potter
1974	VCR#17/ DDR#17	Doubled edge on the east side of the building on the left.		Ken Potter
1974	VCR#18/ DDR#18	Minor, but visible remnants of the first hubbing impression between the two buildings above the ox.		Ken Potter
1974	VCR#19/ DDR#19	Referred to as "Loose barn board" visible above the ox head and horn.		Ken Potters VCR Number via Coins and Canada
1978	DDR	Noticeable extra tree limb between both paddlers on the Reverse.		Coins and Canada
2012-SC	DDO-T1	Most visible on the obverse legends, compare with provided photos.		John O'Connor
2012-SC	DDO-T2	Most visible on the obverse legends, compare with provided photos.		John O'Connor
2012-SC	DDO-T3	Most visible on the obverse legends, compare with provided photos.		John O'Connor
2012-SC	DDO-T4	Most visible on the obverse legends, compare with provided photos.		John O'Connor
2012-SC	DDO-T5	Most visible on the obverse legends, compare with provided photos.		John O'Connor
2012-SC	DDR-T1	Most visible on DOLLAR and CANADA, compare with provided photos.		John O'Connor
2012-SC	DDR-T2	Most visible on DOLLAR and CANADA, compare with provided photos.		John O'Connor
2012-SC	DDO+DDR-T1	Most visible on the obverse and reverse legends, compare with provided photos.		John O'Connor
2012-OL	DDO	Most visible on the obverse legends, compare with provided photos.		John O'Connor
2012-GC	DDO	Most visible on the obverse legends, compare with provided photos.		John O'Connor
2013-SC	DDO-T1	Doubled letters found in ELIZABETH, REGINA and Date. **2013 Canada, & Holiday Sets**		Internet search, was available on eBay
2013-SC	DDR-T1	Doubled letters found in DOLLAR & CANADA. **2013 Canada, & Holiday Sets**		Internet search, was available eBay

		1 DOLLAR REFERENCES CONTINUED		
2013-SC	DDR+DDO-T1	Doubled letters found in DOLLAR & CANADA as well as on the obverse legends and date.		Internet search, was available on eBay
2014-OL	DDR	Doubled "ED" on the bottom left of the reverse for the olympic loon dollar.		John O'Connor
2021-SC	DDR	Doubled neck and earring on the obverse portrait of Queen Elizabeth II.		John O'Connor
2021-KNC	DDR-T1	First prospector, doubled hat and back. Smaller prospector, doubled hat, back, rear leg, and pan.		John O'Connor
2021-KNC	DDR-T2	Large prospector shows a doubled rim on his hat and pan, Smaller prospector has a doubled foot.		John O'Connor
2021-KC	DDR	Large prospector shows a doubled hat, his hand, and his back.		Jonny Gauvin
2022-SC	DDO	Similar to the 2021 Security Loon DDO.		John O'Connor
2022-SC	DDR	Doubled tree limbs on the Reverse.		John O'Connor

2 DOLLARS: 2011 - 2021

DATE	VARIETY	COMMENTS	SOURCE/LINK
2011	DDR-T1	Doubled CANADA and the number 2 on the reverse. *** Test Coin with Polar Bear***	Internet search, was available on eBay
2012-SC	DDO-T1	Doubled REGINA and Date.	John O'Connor
2012-SC	DDO-T2	Doubled ELIZABETH and Date.	John O'Connor
2012-SC	DDO-T3	Doubled digits visible below the date 2012 on the obverse.	Coins and Canada #2359
2012-SC	DDR-T1	Doubled CANADA & DOLLARS.	John O'Connor
2012-SC	DDR+DDO-T1	Rev shows Doubled CANADA & DOLLARS, Obv shows doubled Date and ELIZABETH.	John O'Connor
2012-HMS	DDO-T1	Visible doubled 2012, Leaf with 1812 and ELIZABETH.	Jonny Gauvin
2013-SC	DDR-T1	Doubled DOLLAR & CANADA. **2013 Canada, & Holiday Sets**	Internet search, was available on eBay
2013-SC	DDR+DDO-T1	Doubled DOLLAR & CANADA, doubled obverse legends and date. **2013 Canada, & Holiday Sets**	Internet search, was available on eBay
2021	DDO-T1	Doubled neck and earring on the obverse portrait of Queen Elizabeth II.	John O'Connor

www.ingramcontent.com/pod-product-compliance
Lightning Source LLC
Chambersburg PA
CBHW042025100526
44587CB00029B/4298